WHIS[...]
IN THE
STORM

a true story

ELIZABETH
MOLL STALCUP

Healing Center
INTERNATIONAL

WHISPERS IN THE STORM

ॐ

I DON'T GET OUT MUCH THESE DAYS, but when I do, people ask, "How is Sam?" Then they shake their heads and say, "You two have gone through so much!"

The question, "How is Sam?" is easy to answer. Sam is well. He has gone from spending almost all his time in bed in mid-January to being out of bed all day, able to walk around like you or me. His balance is great. He can go up and down the stairs. He has even gone out a bit—to a grief support group in Fairfax, to a revival prayer meeting in Vienna, to a Leadership Development group in Arlington. His spirits are good. He is no longer anxious. He is back to being the same positive, loveable guy we all know. He enjoys visits and phone calls.

He is taking care of himself and his only restriction is that he can't cook using the stove or oven. And, oh yes, he is tethered to a noisy machine by a 50-foot-long green tube. I nearly forgot about that. He is on oxygen while his lungs heal. Most of the time his oxygen saturation numbers (the measurement of the oxygen levels in his blood at an extremity, in his case, a finger) are great. Sometimes they drop when he exerts himself.

We are grateful to God for bringing us through. And we are believing that God will continue to heal Sam in the days and weeks ahead. We have learned so much. I hope you will make a cup of tea, find a comfy chair and take time to read the inspiring story— my response to the many comments about our suffering—of how God brought us through the perfect storm of life and death, family dynamics, and Immanuel all rolled into one. It happened so fast. For those who last saw us last in November, the change seems bewildering. "What happened to Sam?" a friend recently asked at the April revival prayer meeting.

To us November seems a million miles away. Our story goes even further back to February 2016, when a routine blood test showed that something was slightly off with Sam's blood. The doctor did not seem concerned but ordered follow up tests every three months. The ones in May and August were the same. *A little off.*

By November something was clearly wrong. A bone marrow biopsy showed that Sam had MDS, myelodysplastic syndrome. When you have MDS, your bone marrow is making wonky blood cells. It is as if your bone marrow factory which manufactures blood cells in three flavors, red, white and platelets, is still making blood, but the blood it is making is defective—too big, or misshapen, or missing some key component. One doctor described it this way: imagine if your bone marrow manufactured toasters and is now making them without slots for bread or power cords. Superficially they look useful, but they are not.

During 2017, Sam went through four kinds of chemo and eventually had a bone marrow transplant, receiving healthy 26-year-old marrow from our lovely daughter Sarah. *Drum roll, please!*

At the one-year anniversary of the transplant, August 23, 2018, Sam was given a clean bill of health and taken off all medications that were protecting him from illnesses while his immune system matured: anti-viral, anti-bacterial and anti-fungal. He looked and felt fantastic. We were giddy with delight.

Within a month he had developed a strange dry cough, tight and shallow. I wondered, *Why is he coughing?* It was not productive, more like a short bark. "I've been married to you for 32 years and I have never heard you cough like this. What is going on?" I asked. He shrugged his shoulders and it passed from our minds.

It did not seem important. Then he started lying down on the sofa to nap in the afternoon and being winded when we climbed the hill by our house on our morning walks. His walking partner noted that Sam had "lost the spring in his step" and seemed breathless.

One night, while lying half-awake in bed, I hear a voice shouting in my head, *Pneumonia*. The voice is not audible, yet it can best be described as a shout. I sit upright and look at Sam's sleeping form. *Should I wake him?* I lie back down and roll over.

The next morning, I google the symptoms. Dry cough. Check. Fatigue. Check. Breathlessness on exertion. Check. Pain when you take a deep breath. Check.

"I think you should go see a doctor," I say.

Silence.

I press him. I get strident. No response.

I know Sam has an appointment in dermatology on November 26th. "Why don't you see if someone will see you while you are in the medical center?" I urge.

Sam was not seen that day, but the next day he went to see an internist. When he came home, he reported, "She says I have a virus and to come back in two weeks if I am not better."

"A virus?" I repeat, shaking my head. "A virus does not come on slowly, by degrees." Earlier that day, as he left for his appointment, I had the thought, *I should go with him*. Now I wish I had gone. Instead I had thought about all the work I had to do and sat down in front of my computer.

"Did you tell her that you had had a bone marrow transplant?" I ask.

"Yes."

"Did you tell her that there is a nasty pneumonia you can get from a bone marrow transplant?"

"No."

"Did you tell her it hurts to breathe?

"No, it doesn't hurt to breathe."

"You've told me before that it hurts to breathe. What do you feel when you take a deep breath?"

"I feel like I have to cough."

"Does it feel tight?"

"Yes, tight."

"You need to go back, Sam. I think you might have pneumonia."

By now I am getting triggered. One of my squishy spots is feeling that no one hears me or believes me. I fall into hopeless nagging that screams, *No one EVER believes me!*

Sam refuses to go back. I suspect he does not want to be a nuisance and feels he can just wait it out until the two weeks elapse.

Five days later, on Sunday, December 2nd, I come downstairs ready to go to church. Sam is sitting on the sofa, shoes and jacket on.

"I don't think I feel well enough to go," he says.

"Really?" He had not said anything earlier about feeling unwell.

"No." He lies down.

I take his temperature. 100.4. Elevated but not high.

I let him sleep for a bit but as soon as he stirs, I begin lobbying to go to urgent care.

"I don't want to go to urgent care. Let me rest. If I am still sick on Monday, I will go see my regular doctor."

He agrees to email his doctor. Here is what he writes:

> I was in last week and Dr. R saw me. I think my lungs were clear and bloodwork seemed okay but I'm still feeling pretty punk. I wake up coughing and when I breathe deeply there is pressure and I need to cough. I have been having the shivers. I've taken my temperature and it doesn't seem to be high, maybe 99.
>
> I'm getting pretty winded when I walk. I just don't have a lot of energy and capacity.
>
> I am feeling lethargic. Seems like something is going on but I don't know what it is. Betsy thinks I might have walking pneumonia.

We spend the day resting. I journal, play the piano, and work a few pieces into the jigsaw puzzle. I make dinner but Sam eats little.

The next morning, December 3rd, I ask Sam to make the promised doctor's appointment after 3:00 PM so I can go with him.

I walk our dog with John and Judy, then hurry off to Truro for Leadership Development. While there I listen to God saying:

> *You are a little sad that Sam is sick. You hope that Sam will recover. You are afraid this is serious. I understand how much fear you have about your husband's health. Now that he has*

survived MDS you wonder about other kinds of illnesses. He seems so frail. I have him! Even now I know the exact moment of his departure. It is not soon. I will prepare you. You can trust me. I am always glad to be with you. ALWAYS GLAD! I never get tired of listening to you. I never get tired of guiding you. You do not overwhelm me. You are neither too much nor too little. Let me order your steps. Let me empower you to do all I am calling you to do. Continue to write out prayers in accordance to my will, then place the person in my hands. I love you so much and I delight in every aspect of you.

Every time I take time to engage with God, my soul is restored and I calm down. I feel his peace and presence. I feel loved and safe.

As I drive home I check messages to see when Sam has booked the appointment. At a red light I see a text message that says, "I am feeling better so I did not make a doctor's appointment."

By the time I get home he is back on the sofa, feverish. I sit on the sofa with him with his feet on my lap. He had pulled out a box of Christmas decorations and had set up a few pieces of our creche, then retreated to the sofa.

He also had heard from one of the nurses by email.

"What did it say?" I ask.

"Don't come back until two weeks have elapsed."[1]

---

[1] Sadly, I did not read the actual email until April, four months later. When I did, I realized that the nurse wrote that the doctor had offered Sam a chest x-ray at the original appointment on November 27. The nurse also offered another appointment or a chest x-ray in the email. When I asked Sam about this, he seemed surprised and did not remember being offered a chest x-ray or an appointment, yet there it was.

"Sam, I think you need to go back."

The next morning Sam is asleep when I get up. When I go back upstairs an hour later, he is lying in bed looking at his phone. For months we have been working with my coach Maritza on codependency, my tendency to be over-responsible as well as Sam's tendency to be under-responsible. Despite the progress we have made, at the point I have reached my limit. "Right now!" I order. "Right now, call the doctor and make an appointment. I'm going with you. Any time. Just do it."

By 10:45 we are in the doctor's office. "His lungs still sound clear," she reports. His oxygen saturation levels are down to 90% and his temperature is a little over 100.

I ask the doctor, "Are you aware that there is a bad kind of pneumonia that you can get when you've had a bone marrow transplant?"

"No, I wasn't."

I glare at her. I am angry. I am angry at Sam for not going back to the doctor earlier. I am angry at myself for not going with him the first time. I am angry at the doctor for misdiagnosing him.

She sends him down for a chest x-ray.

The diagnosis: bilateral pneumonia. *Yikes! Both sides of the lungs!* She prescribes two kinds of oral antibiotics and sends him home to rest. *At last*, I think! *At last someone is listening to me. Now he will get better fast.*

But I was wrong. I had no idea what we were up against.

At bedtime, after two doses of antibiotics his fever is 101.5. We go to bed trusting Sam will show some signs of improvement in the morning.

That night I talk to God who says, *I ordained that he would be diagnosed on this day.*

"Oh Lord," I cry. "When I heard the word pneumonia, I didn't realize it was you. I would have had more peace. I am sad that Sam is sick." Then God speaks to my mind: *He will not die. I am wanting you to be more confident and bold.*

I realize that I should have gone back to God and asked, "Is that you?" when I first hear the word pneumonia. Instead I focused on trying to talk Sam into my point of view. If I had been more confident I was hearing from God, I would have approached Sam from a place of confidence.

On Wednesday I go out early to walk our dog with my friend Judy. As I am driving home around 9 AM, I call Sam to see if he is up, hoping, expecting, to hear that he is improving.

"Kaiser called to see if I was feeling better," he reports. "I'm not feeling better, maybe even worse. They want me to come to urgent care immediately."

"Okay. I'm ten minutes away. Get ready. I'll take you right in."

At urgent care they do all the normal preliminaries and then put him on two IV antibiotics. His O_2 levels are now 88%, so they give him oxygen through a nasal cannula.

Now, I think. *Now Sam will recover quickly.*

We wait and wait for a recovery that never comes.

At lunch I walk over to Harris Teeter and buy food.

We wait and wait for Sam to feel better.

In late afternoon the doctor says, "We may need to keep him overnight, so he can stay on IV meds longer and get better more quickly." It seems like a good plan. I urge the doctor to reach out to Sam's transplant doctor, Dr. Luznik, at Johns Hopkins and talk to him about the possible link to Sam's bone marrow transplant, but I can tell the doctor thinks I am meddling in topics about which I know little.

I dial Dr. Luznik myself, but there's no answer, so I leave a message asking him to call me back.

I kiss Sam and leave him to sleep.

At home, I finish my take-home exam for seminary and submit it online.

I look up the kind of pneumonia that can afflict people after a bone marrow transplant.

Pneumocystis. I read about how this kind of pneumonia killed so many people with AIDS in the early years. It sounds as if it was almost always fatal. *Oh Lord!*

I call Sam to pray with him at bedtime but do not tell him what I have learned. I know from past experience that he would not want to know. In the middle of the night I awake and begin to fret. Could Sam have pneumocystis pneumonia?

During the months at Johns Hopkins, I had begun to practice Immanuel Journaling[2] in the middle of the night using my phone to record my interactions with God. In the wee hours of the morning of December 6th, I record:

---

[2] You can learn more about Immanuel Journaling here: https://bit.ly/2JfldoA or https://bit.ly/2Jcf1xP

Lord, I am grateful that you are stronger than any disease.

In my mind, I heard God's response to my gratitude: *I am bigger than the universe and stronger than the force of gravity. I am intimately aware of every detail of your life and everything that is going on in Sam's body.*

God continued to speak to me: *I see you propped up in bed. You're a little cold. The room is dark and you are alone because Sam is in urgent care. You can't decide if you should get up and go there now at 5 AM or if you should try to get more sleep.*

I hear you. You are afraid that he is going to die. You are afraid that his anxiety is affecting his breathing. You are afraid that they aren't treating this correctly. You were frustrated when the doctor didn't seem interested in calling Johns Hopkins to find out more. You are frightened by the research articles that you read last night that seemed to indicate that this kind of pneumonia is almost always fatal.

I know how big this is for you. The thought of losing your husband or having him be brain-damaged through lack of oxygen is truly terrifying. You're not sure what to believe—the sense that both of you were going to live into your 90s or the sense that he had two years to live.[3] I want to remind you, dear one, that I said you had at least two years. It was meant to comfort

---

[3] In December 2016 when Sam was newly diagnosed with MDS, I heard God say that Sam would live two years. This was both a comfort because I knew he would not die right away but also a source of great sorrow. I had also heard earlier that Sam and I would both live into our 90s, so I was confused about how these two seemly contradictory words of knowledge would come together. The pneumonia described here came two years after Sam was first diagnosed with MDS.

you when he was first diagnosed, and you were afraid he would die suddenly. I will bring both of you through this. I am at work on so many levels in you, in him, in your community. Let me take care of him. Even now he is surrounded by my holy angels and they are ministering to him.

I am leading you. I know the way and I go before you. I led you to call Dr. Luznik. I spoke to you and told you that Sam had pneumonia. I led you to go to the doctor with him.

I am at work in his body and I will restore him. Dear one, get more sleep. Trust me. My timing is perfect. Do not be afraid that you will miss out on my will. You are easy to lead.

I let God comfort me and go back to sleep.

In the morning Sam wakes me early, "They are transferring me to a hospital."

I am surprised and want to know more. He does not know why, just that they want him to be hospitalized. I pack some shirts and sports shorts for Sam and a few toiletries and drive to the urgent care center at Tysons.

The doctor on call listens to my theory that this pneumonia is related to Sam's bone marrow transplant. "What you are saying makes sense," he responds thoughtfully. *At last,* I think, *I've convinced a medical professional,* but later I learned that he had reached out to an infectious disease doctor during the night when Sam continued to decline. "If he has had a bone marrow transplant," the specialist had said, "you need to get him to a hospital."

By 4:00 PM on December 6th, Sam is in room 730 at Virginia Hospital Center. Now he has a whole new set of doctors, including

Dr. Pic, the stylish Romanian who had ordered him to the hospital. She takes Dr. Luznik's number and promises to call.

A few hours later, Dr. Luznik calls me.

"Where do you see this going?" I ask.

"I am not sure. I understand he nearly needs life support. Some people recover." He pauses, then continues. "If only we had gotten him a week earlier."

I touch the wall to steady myself. *A week earlier.* His words stab me. He is a kind man and does not know that a week earlier, I was crying out, alone, with no one to hear my cry. How could Sam have gone downhill so fast? Only four days have elapsed since he lay down on the sofa, feverish.

Dr. Luznik closes the call by urging me to get our people praying. *That I can do.*

At the end of the day, I send an update to my intercessors, 47 people, some of whom had been praying for us for years. I update them about what is happening to Sam and then list what I am grateful for:

- I'm grateful that I figured out the parking machine at Virginia Hospital Center.

- I'm grateful that Sam got a room in the hospital instead of being transferred to the emergency room.

- I am grateful that his Vietnamese nurse, Lilly, seems very sweet, and is a believer.

- I am grateful that my friends John and Judy have picked up our dog so I don't have to worry about Darby.

- I am grateful for all of you who are praying for us.

The next day, December 7th, Sam's oxygen saturation is between 83 and 84%—way too low. They turn his oxygen up to 100%. I can read panic in his eyes. He cannot talk with the mask on but his O₂ numbers come up.

Oh Lord, is this really happening?

The first few days in the hospital we watch in horror as the staff turns up the level of oxygen flowing into Sam's lungs every few hours only to watch his saturation levels decline. We are glued to the monitor that takes the readings.

Sam's fight to breathe is creating a perfect storm for anxiety to bloom. I cannot avert my eyes. By now our son, Sammy, has joined me and our daughter, Sarah, is on the way. We are gripped by the intensity of his suffering.

I am terrified but I am also angry. Angry at everything and every-one who has brought us to this terrifying juncture. Sam. Me. The first doctor. My anger is impacting my relationships with every-one, including God. I cannot hear God over the rumble of my an-ger. Anger occupies such a deep rut in my brain that not even a Mack Anthem semi-truck—the most powerful truck in the world—can power out of its depths.

"Lord," I cry, "I am so angry! It feels like I have a right to be angry, but I don't want to be stuck here. I give the anger to you and ask you to lift it off me."

God does. Then he gently reminds me to stop talking about it, stop nursing the hurt and pain. I know that it is important to acknowledge my anger, but I also know that I am not to hang on to it. It is too much for me. I have to surrender it to him. It is the only way.

I focus on small gifts. The bench seating in Sam's hospital room is flooded by nourishing winter sun. It warms my back in the chilly room. Sam is working so hard to breathe that he always feels hot. He has the room thermostat on the lowest setting and no blankets on his legs. When visitors come, they start to take off their winter coats, then slip them back on.

Amazingly at times, Sam emerges from the battle and chats with the doctors, respiratory therapists, and nurses. The staff love him. He wants to know where they are from and if they have a family. His bright shining eyes communicate so much warmth and genuine interest. They love being in his room. The rest of us keep the conversations going when Sam is unable to talk. You can tell that Sam enjoys hearing about the lives of everyone involved in his care.

One of the respiratory therapists, a woman from Ethiopia, coaches Sam to "smell the roses and blow out the candles." I try to coach Sam too, and at times I imagine it is helping, but looking back I think I only made him more anxious since he could not comply with my instructions. I realize with sorrow that most of the calming exercises we teach at Healing Center International involve breathing slowly and deeply, something that is impossible for Sam. He cannot take a deep breath. Instead his stomach muscles roll like the ocean in a desperate attempt to get air into his lungs. At times he taps his chest, stimulating his vagus nerves. I try to work with him, to help him process what he is experiencing, but all I learn is that he is afraid of dying.

The team of four doctors who are seeing him keep switching his antibiotics and anti-fungals. Levaquin. Bactrim. Cresemba. Vancomycin. Dioxin. Voriconazole.

People show up to visit Sam, but often their presence makes him frantic. His eyes widen and follow their every move. As a consummate extrovert, he wants to talk, wants to make them feel at home, but he can't. It is all he can do to get air into his lungs. Time after time, I have to escort people out or intercept them at the door and ask them to leave. I know they think I am the one who doesn't want visitors because it is hard to imagine Sam not wanting them, but I do not care what they think. I have to protect my husband.

Now that I can see how sick he is, I am filled with remorse. *I should have gone with him to that first appointment. I should have made him go back sooner.* I talk to God who comforts me by saying, *I am so much bigger than your mistakes.*

Friday, December 7, 2018

The second day in the hospital I follow Dr. Pic out of Sam's room. I have questions, but I do not want to ask her in front of him. My first is, "Where is this going?"

"We will probably need to move him to ICU so we can intubate him."

Her eyes meet mine. Steady. I instinctively know she is telling me the truth.

"That is so sad," I say.

"Yes, it is," she replies.

"Do you think he has PCP?"[4] I ask. *How could he have it? By now his immune system should be stronger.*

"I think he contracted this in the summer of 2017 when he had chemo," she answers.

---

[4] PCP is the shorthand term for Pneumocystis.

I remembered the time. He was in the hospital for a month that summer getting three kinds of strong chemo. He needed the chemo to bring him into remission so he could get a bone marrow transplant. He became desperately ill following the chemo during the nadir.[5] Despite many tests the doctors never figured out what was making him so sick. His white blood cell count was so low that that alone can make you susceptible to all kinds of bugs. The only suspects they identified were some spots in his lungs. The spots later decreased in size and Sam was cleared for the bone marrow transplant.

I realize what she was saying. If he contracted PCP back in July of 2017, and it was kept at bay by the antibiotics and antifungals he took from August 2017 to August 2018, then that would explain why it was taking hold now, more than a year after the transplant.

"So you think he has PCP?" I ask.

"I know he does," she responds.

I ponder the realization that although it is easy to fear truth, once it is out, it resonates and makes us stronger. I did not want to be afraid of the truth. I remember how God warned the Apostle Paul about his coming imprisonment. I know God was preparing my heart.

Dr. Pic also lets me know that the team who is treating Sam needs to agree on a diagnosis and they can only get that from a bronchoscopy, where they thread a tiny scope into Sam's lungs, take a tissue sample, and wash a bit of his lungs, then suck out the fluid which would contain some of the germs.

---

[5] A nadir is the low point that occurs after the chemo is administered. It can last days to weeks.

Dr. Pic feels they should do a bronchoscopy now; other doctors feel that Sam is too unstable.

"If we intubate him," she says, "we will be able to do it."

I know that intubation has its own risks—that not all who are intubated recover. It is impossible to know how to pray except, *Lord have mercy on us!*

Sunday, December 9

Sam seems incredibly anxious. When I get to the hospital a little after 9 AM, I try to help him calm down by coaching him to "smell the roses and blow out the candles." But neither Sammy nor I can calm him down. He shifts his position in the bed, grabs the oxygen tubing under his chin and slides his hand down the length of it to his waist, then grips the side railings on the bed so tightly that the muscles on his arms stand out. Then he repeats those movements: shift, grab, slide, grip.

It is exhausting to watch as the hours tick by.

The doctors are making their rounds. Dr. Pic, Dr. Dutta, the hospitalist, and Dr. Decker, the pulmonologist. Each one notices Sam's distress. Dr. Pic had been lobbying for a bronchoscopy.

"He's too unstable to have a bronchoscopy," Dr. Decker says.

After the doctors are finished, Sam, Sammy, and I celebrate the Eucharist together.

We order a chicken salad sandwich for Sam, but he does not touch it—though he does eat a chocolate chip cookie sent by his cousin.

By 2:30 PM he is pulling hard to breathe. The sound of his breathing fills our heads.

The nurse comes in to report that his blood pressure, monitored in a little room on the floor, is now 180/80. His breathing becomes even more labored.

The nurse calls Dr. Dutta. Within five minutes medical personnel crowd the room: a nurse from ICU with a clipboard, the respiratory therapist, a huge black man, and Sam's regular nurse, Jen. Within minutes Dr. Decker joins them. As the pulmonologist, he is in charge.

The lady with the clipboard begins asking questions. Each specialist answers. Sam's eyes widen and fill with fear and his saturation numbers begin to drop even further.

"Get him to ICU," Dr. Decker orders.

The woman lowers her clipboard, and glares at him, "So much for protocol!" she fumes.

"I didn't want to watch him . . ." Dr. Decker's voice trails off.

Immediately, someone unlocks the bed and begins rolling it down the hallway. I had been trying to gather our things, but I drop the bag of dirty clothes and grab hold of the top left bed rail and sprint alongside. Behind me is a short nurse I have not seen before. I glance back to see if she looks familiar and see that she has placed an oblong box on Sam's bed next to his legs. The box is labeled "paddles." On the other side of the bed is the tall, broad-shouldered respiratory therapist (so good to have someone familiar) and another nurse.

As we move swiftly down the hallway, all four with a hand on the rail, the nurse behind me says, "We might not have room for you in the elevator."

Part of me wants to give up, to curl into a ball in the hallway and wail but another part of me does not falter and keeps up the pace.

The nurse on the other side of the bed says, "We can squeeze her in."

We wheel the bed into the elevator, the two nurses and I pressed against the wall with the bed up tight against our bellies while the respiratory therapist takes the other side.

Five flights down and we are out in the hallway, through a double door and into his room, 27, one over from the door.

Yet another unfamiliar nurse approaches, "Are you family?"

"Yes."

"Would you give us ten minutes to get him settled?"

"No, I can't leave him. I promised." I know Sam could die at any moment. "I won't get in the way."

She lets me pass. I press against the wall at the foot of the bed, and call out to Sam, "Honey, I am here!"

He looks up. Frozen. Overwhelmed.

With perfect synchronicity, one of the nurses calls out orders: "Side." In perfect unison, they turn Sam on his side, quickly check his bottom for bedsores and slide a body-sized mylar sheet under him. "Back." In unison they roll him onto the sheet. "Slide." They slide the sheet with Sam atop it from his old bed to his new bed in ICU.

"Sam, I am here," I call out.

He looks calmer. Nothing has happened except that we are now in ICU.

"He looks better," I comment.

"Yes," one of the nurses quips. "It's the magic elevator ride."

Soon they are placing a BiPAP[6] mask on his face and he is breathing. *Thank God he was used to using a CPAP for sleep apnea.* I had been told that not all people tolerated a BiPAP. If the BiPAP did not work, they would have to intubate him. They give him something for anxiety. For the first time in many days, I see Sam take a single unified breath as the machine forces air into his lungs. *Thank you, Jesus!* Within a short time he is asleep. It is the first time he has slept in four days.

When I see him sleeping, I am overwhelmed by fatigue. I pull a chair close and drop my arms and head onto a corner of the bed.

Medical personnel are going in and out, checking vitals, asking questions.

"Please," I ask, "Can you leave him alone for a bit? He has not slept in four days." To my surprise, they say yes and leave the room.

It is 4:00 PM.

By now Sammy and Sarah had found their way to Sam's room, and had arrived bearing bags of belongings. Thank God for my

---

[6] "A BiPAP is a mode of respiratory ventilation that can be used for those who are critically ill in hospital with respiratory failure. The "PAP" stands for "Positive Airway Pressure." A CPAP has one pressure setting while a BiPAP has two—one for inhalation and one for exhalation. The dual settings allow the patient to get more air in and out of their lungs." Wikipedia, Positive Airway Pressure, accessed 4/16/2019.

adult children! The nurse found an extra chair and we settled in with our computer bags, winter coats, Sam's clean and dirty clothes, and food. The ICU room was much smaller and lacked cabinets. Some of our belongings were taken down to our cars parked beneath us in the parking garage. Then we all dozed as best we could.

Sam slept for 36 hours.

I realized during our time in ICU that often what we fear the most is the way forward. ICU was exactly what Sam needed at that moment.

When Sam was admitted to the hospital, I felt that we should not leave him. He needed to have someone with him with whom he had a secure attachment, a strong bond. I told my adult children that I could be there all day, but I needed them to spend the night with their dad. We also tried to think of friends and family with whom Sam shared a deep bond.

That first night in ICU, our son Sammy stayed with him. They next night Sam's brother Dana came and slept on the uncomfortable chair that unfolded to make a somewhat flat surface.

I was astonished to see how many people in ICU were alone. Unlike the hospital floor, the wall between the room and the hallway in ICU is glass, with thin curtains for privacy. You could not help but see into every room as you walked down the hallway to get a cup of hot water or heat your noodles. Most of the patients were completely alone.

Tuesday, December 11

When I get in that morning, Sam seems a bit anxious. They have taken him off the BiPAP and are trying the high-flow nasal cannula at reduced oxygen levels.

Sam gets a lot more attention in ICU. His anxiety and breathing are much better. For the first time since he entered the ICU, they let him eat and drink water. They have been holding back in hopes that he would be stable enough to tolerate a bronchoscopy. He is too unstable, so they let him eat and drink.

As the day wears on, the medical personnel keep trying to gradually turn down the amount of oxygen until Sam begins to struggle, and then they turn it back up. He is still not considered stable, but they believe the pneumonia is being defeated because he is able to tolerate lower oxygen levels than before.

Roxy brings her mom's Chilean cooking for lunch. It is good to see her face and eat delicious food.

By now my daughter Sarah is here too. It is so good to have Sarah and Sammy with me. I can see by the look on his face that Sam is encouraged by their presence too. He is so vulnerable now. Having two of his three children with him buoys him up.

At 8:00 PM, Sarah and I go back to Jeannie and Jerry's home, less than a mile from the hospital. Before I fall asleep, I send an update to my intercessors from my phone while lying in bed:

> We are grateful for your prayers. We are also wearing a little thin, and I think Sarah feels like she needs to return to med school. She's pretty stressed about all she is missing. We would appreciate prayers for her, especially for wisdom to know whether she should take an incomplete in one of her classes. She would have to finish it before school begins in January which would be very challenging but may be the best decision.
>
> Thank you for praying for all of us.

We are grateful that Jerry and Jeannie have opened their home to us again!

We are grateful to Sam's cousin and his wife who also live nearby. Some of us have stayed there as well.

We are grateful that John and Judy are taking care of our dog, and so far someone has brought us lunch and dinner every day. It has been amazing especially since the hospital is super crowded around lunchtime and parking is nearly impossible to find.

We are grateful for the Lord. We are grateful for Jay and Eleni who came and prayed for us today.

We are grateful for Roxy who brought us lunch.

We are grateful for Sammy's boss who is giving him time off and for Sarah's med school which has also been very understanding.

It seems that there is a tsunami of people praying for us.

We are thankful. We are grateful for all of your kind notes. We read them all, but don't have the bandwidth to reply to all of them.

Love,

B.

Wednesday, December 12

Sam is still in ICU. He had trouble with the BiPAP during the night. It seemed out of sync with his breathing. He is supposed to have a bronchoscopy tomorrow. At last. Maybe. If he seems to be doing well, they will put him on the list. He can't eat or drink before.

Today is quiet. The respiratory therapist figured out how to make the BiPAP work better for Sam.

Eleni brings an entire bag of food from Moby Dick. Yummy! We eat it for lunch and dinner.

At 4:00 PM one of the ICU doctors comes into Sam's room and says that it would be helpful if he had a copy of the CT scan taken by Kaiser at their urgent care facility on December5th.

"Can't you ask for it and have them send it to you?" I ask.

"I know it doesn't seem logical, but the fastest way for us to get our hands on it is for you to request it and go get it," replies the doctor.

I know the bronchoscopy is important in diagnosing the pneumonia, but it is also risky. I picture the scan helping the doctors guide the scope.

"Okay," I say, jumping up. "I am on it." Then I pause. *What to do?* "Sarah can you come with me?" I ask.

"Yes."

Sarah and I grab our bags and are headed out the door when I realize that Sammy's car might be closer, parked on the street instead of deep within the bowels of the parking garage.

"Sammy, are you parked on the street?"

"Yes," he says, looking up. Sammy had spent the night with Sam and has remained with him all day. Several times I had suggested that he leave since he was exhausted.

"We don't need three people here during the day," I had said earlier.

"I'm going to stay until five, then leave," he had replied. Then he brought up the uncomfortable complaint for the second or third time. "Why aren't you taking a turn staying with Dad overnight?"

I had announced at the beginning that I would be there every day but would not spend the night as I did not think I could sleep in the hospital and still interact coherently with the doctors during the day. Everyone agreed to this plan until the nights began to take their toll. Then the complaining began.

Sammy is working on his laptop, still intending to leave at 5:00 PM. Now he wants to know, "Could you be back by 5:00?"

I am not sure. It is rush hour, impossible to predict.

I feel my heart beating hard and fast. I do not have time to talk about this. I do not know how late Kaiser is open and where I need to go in the vast medical center to get the CT scan images.

"Don't worry about lending us your car," I decide. "We can take mine. I don't have time to talk to you about this. If you have to go at 5:00 PM, go!"

"But what about Dad?"

"Arggh!" I feel trapped. "I've got to go! He's in ICU where they are keeping a close eye on him. He will be okay if he has to be alone for a short while. We will be back as soon as we can, we've got to go."

"But do you need to take Sarah with you?"

"Yes, I need her."

"Why?"

"I don't have time to talk about this."

Sammy gives me a look that says, *once again Mom is refusing to talk about hard stuff.* For some time, I had been behaving like a possum. Hurt when I was accused of exaggerating or being overly negative. Not wanting anyone to know how much it hurt. Avoiding conflict.

Sarah and I rush out. It seems an eternity as we wait for the elevator to the lobby, then the elevator to the garage. At last we are in the car, Sarah at the wheel. I don't know how to get to Kaiser from Virginia Hospital Center and I need to call Kaiser. *What to do first?*

I direct Sarah onto 66 west and then call Kaiser. The woman who answers the phone doesn't know where to send my call, so I talk in turn with urgent care, Radiology, and at last Member Services where I am connected with a kind and gracious woman.

Her soft, unhurried voice calms me. "Yes, I can access that data and burn a disc now. But can you get here in time to pick it up? We close at 5:00 PM."

"Yes," I say confidently, though I feel anything but confident. Traffic is lighter than I had feared, but we aren't there yet. Still it seems that God is going before us and ordering our steps.

At 4:45 Sarah pulls into the parking lot. I direct her up and around the garage to the second floor where the ramp is on the same level as the medical center. I bolt from the car and sprint into Member Services, which is thankfully right inside the front door. I am moving fast until I run smack into a long line of people. *Oh no,* I think, feeling panicky. *I hope they don't close while people are still waiting!* In a few short minutes, I am at the window ready to grab the disc and run. I can see it sitting on the counter.

"Please fill out this release," the receptionist says handing me a clipboard. *Whoa!* I take a deep breath and step away from the window and back in line. I scribble out the answers while waiting. When I finish, I want to explain to everyone in line in front of me that I only have to trade the form on my clipboard for a CD and can I maybe move up a bit? A kindly man puts me in my place, "Honey, everybody else is doing the same thing!" I docilely step back in line.

Soon I have the disc. I feel euphoric. Sarah and I are the heroes! Still pumped with adrenaline, I scoot out to the car and climb in. Now, how to get back?

We follow Google Maps through the back streets of Tysons Corner, Falls Church, and Arlington. We make what seems like at least 40 turns. The sun sets. Christmas lights come on. We call Sammy. It is long past five but he is still there and has calmed down. He is willing to wait.

"Mom I want to talk about this some time."

"Yes," I say, hoping that day will never come.

Friday, December 14

I am there early the next morning. They are already prepping Sam for his long-awaited bronchoscopy.

One of our kids says something that feels unkind. I try to catch my emotional balance but then feel nauseous, so I bolt from the room, crying. I do not want to upset Sam, so I leave. I am afraid I will vomit if I pause to explain.

Once I get out of ICU, I search for a quiet corner, but the second-floor balcony and seating area are packed. I automatically keep moving and find myself next to my car in the parking garage. I get in and begin driving. Suddenly, I am overcome by a desire to go home. I call my friend Sarah from the car and she listens, attuning well. As I near home, we agree that I will call her back in ten minutes. I lug my bags inside, start the washing machine, then sit on the white sofa and call her back. She does HeartSync[7] with me. Being home is comforting and stabilizing, and getting HeartSync calms my anxious, hurting parts.

After a few hours at home I head back to the hospital. Sam has successfully come through the bronchoscopy, but we won't have results for a few more days.

For the first time no one spends the night with Sam.

Saturday, December 15

When I arrive in the morning, Sam is very anxious, breathing both fast and out-of-sync while on 80% oxygen. They had warned us that he might take a turn for the worse after the bronchoscopy. The respiratory therapist tries the BiPAP, but what had once been so life-giving no longer works for Sam. He has a sense that the machine is not in sync with his breathing. The BiPAP only tires him. I try coaching him, "Smell the roses, blow out the candles." It seems to help him breathe better but after one hour he wants off the BiPAP and when I question him, he says my coaching wore him out.

Sad.

---

[7] HeartSync is a method of inner healing founded by Canon Andrew Miller. For more info, go to https://bit.ly/307nesk

Today is the day of the Healing Center International Christmas Tea, our annual fundraiser. I am not going to attend because by now it is just me and my son Sammy, who is slated to be one of our speakers.

About 4:00 PM Sammy comes in with a good report from the tea. Wonderful testimonies. Delicious food. A beautiful venue, the stately Regent House in Annandale. Tables with cloth table-cloths, china, and teapots. Sammy has always been an enthusiastic supporter of our ministry and, not surprisingly, Chaney says he represented the Stalcup family well.

Now that Sammy is back at the hospital, I ask if I can leave, not knowing where I want to go.

Sammy offers his car, which is on the street. I ask which street but he is not sure of the name. "The one that is that way," he says, pointing in the direction of George Mason Road. *Or so I thought.* I head outside but cannot find it. It is raining heavily and I have no umbrella. I am wearing a raincoat but my head is getting soaked.

I had called my friend Anne as I left the building to ask if I could come visit.

"Yes, I am in the car on my way home. I just got to my exit. I will be there in ten minutes."

I search George Mason Road for Sammy's silver Prius without finding it. I walk to the corner and look down 16th Street. *Is that the car?* About ten cars from the corner, I find the car and climb in. Then immediately I feel disoriented.

Hadn't we owned this car just three years ago? I push the power button. Nothing. I remember that the charge on the key fob was weak. I grab my purse, but it proves to be a black hole. I fish around, then start taking out my wallet, two letters, sunglasses, my toothbrush case. There at last are the keys. I put them in the slot and start the car.

I am so wet that the car fogs up inside as I drive with the heat on. My brain seems just as foggy as the car.

What was that? A man darts in front of me and is safely on the other side before I can make sense of what I am seeing in the dark and rain. My heart races at what might have been. At the red light I find Anne's address in my phone and follow the directions through unfamiliar streets: Woodcock, Taylor. It starts to look familiar, then not—turn right then left, now at Old Dominion now right and back on Taylor, Lorcom. It is hard to see in the pelting rain. Left, then up and around. I am there. The house looks dark.

I sit in the car and google PCP—it is exactly what Sam has. A pneumonia caused by germs that are all around us and are only dangerous to those with weakened immune systems, like those stricken with AIDS. I'm not sure why I am so confident, but I know that I know.

"It can be fatal," I read. I know that already, by watching someone I love fight it. *Sam is in God's hands.*

In my rearview mirror, I see Anne pull into her garage. I meet her there and we step into her cozy home through her kitchen door. She greets me warmly, then puts the kettle on and pours out a dish of mixed nuts. We sit in her living room surrounded by treasures from around the world, a testament to her husband's work overseas. Such beauty. Such creativity.

The soft pebbly feel of the familiar white leather sofa. Anne's sweet soft voice and her attunement comfort me. I tell a story from another time, about Howard and his computer woes.[8] Anne listens. It feels good to speak so confidently about a story that was resolved long ago.

Anne needs to leave for church, so our visit is short. She walks me to the door and hands me my now dry raincoat and one of her umbrellas. She hugs me and I go out into the cold rain.

Sammy texts: "ETA?"

"Coming," I text back.

I pull up outside the hospital and walk in.

I tell Sammy that his car had been on 16th Street and describe my search for his car in the rain. In my opinion, from inside Sam's hospital room, Sammy had pointed toward George Mason when the car was actually on 16th. He disagrees as to the direction of the street. *This is crazy.* In our low capacity states, we cannot reconcile our differing points of view. We even walk to where the street below is visible from the second-floor balcony, but cannot agree on which way he had pointed and which street was which.

Back in Sam's room, they decide to try the BiPAP on CPAP mode, since Sam regularly uses a CPAP at home. I do some HeartSync with Sam who is now calm enough to participate.

Later that night, I get this text message from him: "Thanks for the HeartSync. Doing better."

---

[8] Moll-Stalcup, Elizabeth. "How Would I Tell Howard?" *Decision*, August 1997.

Sunday, December 16

Sam is calmer today. John has spent the night with him and has stayed until I could arrive from Jerry and Jeannie's home, just down the street.

We have Stalcup Family Church with apple juice and consecrated hosts. Sweet time.

John leaves.

Sam has slept well with the CPAP but still feels exhausted. He sleeps all morning. Sometimes I think he is asleep, but his eyes are open, looking at me.

We get the results from the bronchoscopy. Sam has PCP, pneumocystis. No one tells me or Dr. Pic, you were right. *Why does this matter to me?*

I think back to Sam's first few days in the hospital. One morning I came in to find the hospitalist explaining to Sam why she did not think he had PCP. Both Sammy and Sam looked elated at the good news. But her pep talk only made me angry.

"Why do you think it is not PCP?" I asked her.

"Well, his fever went down within a few days of getting IV antibiotics," she replied.

"That is not true. He started getting IV antibiotics in urgent care on December 5th. What else?" I asked.

She gave several reasons. I shot them all down. Finally, she admitted that she did not know much about PCP and left the room.

I looked at Sammy and Sam. They looked hurt and confused.

"Why do you always have to be so negative?" Sammy asked.

I had been triggered by the sweet doctor, who I knew meant well, but didn't have her facts straight. It seemed that very few doctors understood PCP. I had noticed that none of them could hear it initially. They would look puzzled as they moved their stethoscopes around Sam's chest, listening.

"You can't hear anything, can you?" I asked one after another.

"No, I can't," was the honest reply.

"Don't worry," I reassured them. "None of the other doctors can either."

I understand now why Dr. R. thought his lungs were clear at that first appointment in November.

But in that moment I was peeved by what I perceived to be the doctor giving Sam false hope. In my triggered state I became non-relational. Sammy's comment about being overly negative triggered me further. I felt not seen, not heard, not understood. Looking back months later, I can see that Sammy's reaction had deep roots. I had a long history of being fearful, of amplifying the situation in the hopes of finding validation. My reaction had deep roots too!

Now, I see that in a life and death situation like this one, everyone is going to get triggered. Small irritations that we could live with before become overwhelming as our "stuff" rises to the surface. No exceptions—except for Jesus! Looking back I can see that being right was important, but not as important as staying relational and tender towards those I love.

Monday, December 17

Sam is now off the BiPAP and on a high-pressure nasal cannula which has two settings, the first for pressure, the second for the oxygen mix. His is set at 35 pressure; 55% O_2.

At 12:40 the respiratory therapist turns it down to 30 pressure and 55% O_2.

Sam now weighs 84 kg or 185 lbs. He weighed 205 lbs when this started.

"Lord, how do you want me to pray for Sam at this time, in this hour?"

Pray that he would know me in his suffering.

Our friend Jerry sits with Sam. He has a calming influence. Sam is sleeping with his mouth open.

I walk around the block with my friend Reid, but it is hard to get my mind off Sam even though I know Jerry is with him. Other than sleeping at night, I have had few breaks. How sweet to be outside.

At 6:00 PM Sam gets wiped down by his nurse, Rabi. I eat Jeannie's good soup.

By the time I leave at 8:00 PM, Sam seems calmer, breathing more evenly with pressure in the low 20s and high teens. Except when he pooed! The first time in eight days—then his heart rate shot up to 150, a little scary.

Earlier, Dr. Wong said Sam had come into the hospital almost needing life support. Just thinking about this is maddening. And terrifying.

That evening at Jeannie's house I watch them get ready to leave for Tampa. I am sad to see them go. Jeannie is always eager to hear what transpired each day, and as a nurse she understands the urgency of our lives without my needing to explain. Talking to her at the end of each day helps me process.

Later that evening I pray: "Lord, I am grateful that you spared my husband's life and that he is slowly getting better."

God's response: *He is in my hands. I am at work. Nothing escapes my notice. I know every detail. I see you sitting on the floor in Jeannie's house. Your back hurts. Now you have moved to the comfy green chair. You feel exhausted but agitated. When Dr. Wong said Sam came in to the hospital nearly needing life support your brain burst into flame! Yikes! Yikes! You cannot get those words out of your mind.*

You are so glad he is breathing steadily today. I am glad to be with you as you struggle with your own anxiety. You can connect to me any time. I am powerful enough to do something about all this: Sarah's class; Sam's health.

Tuesday, December 18

Dana, Sam's youngest brother, has spent the night with him. Sam did not sleep. He says he feels wretched, but the doctors say he is doing better. He has a second bowel movement at 10:00 AM. He is now sleeping, not having slept all night. The ICU doctors are talking about transferring Sam to a step-down unit on the sixth floor.

He needs to eat; to be willing to sit up and stand. He needs to walk to the toilet but needs a walker to get there.

Was he really walking two miles twice a week just three weeks ago? Lord, I do not want to take offense! It is so easy to blame others and myself.

Sam is moved to room 602 in the step-down unit.

His oxygen saturation goes into the 80s when he urinates but is 93% when sleeping.

Wednesday, December 19

Sam slept well after taking a sleeping aid and Xanax. Early in the morning he has chest pain in his sternum area. They find elevated troponin, an enzyme that is released into the blood by dying heart muscles.

I do Immanuel Journaling out loud to still my anxious heart and it seems to help Sam, too.

Dr. Lee says it looks like he might have had a heart attack.

Thursday, December 20

Sam slept well again. John Chab stayed overnight with him. He has chest pain around 10:00 AM again, but it subsides. He is visited by Dr. Yoho, infectious disease, who adds two more antibiotics and takes Sam off Bactrim, because it is hard on the kidneys and Sam's are showing signs of stress. Bactrim is the drug of choice for treating PCP and Dr. Yoho says that Sam tolerated it for eleven days and that it is rare for anyone to tolerate a full dose. He changes him to Modron, a yellow paste in a packet that Sam squeezes into his mouth, like the mustard packets at McDonalds. It looks disgusting but Sam does not seem to mind. It amazes me that Sam does not complain about all the medications he must swallow. He is also taking Cresemba by mouth. Dr. Yoho orders a new chest x-ray.

A cardiologist of Indian descent stops by. He went to Hopkins for undergrad, med school, and residency. He says it was brutal and we believe him! As to Sam's condition, he says that some things suggest that Sam had a heart attack, but others do not. For example, Troponin, the heart enzyme, went up between morning and afternoon.

Dr. Chakurkar, the pulmonologist on-call, says Sam should not be reclining in bed, but should take a one-hour nap and then sit up.

"How high?" I ask her.

"As high as possible."

I look at the bed. Seventy degrees is as high as it will go, but when I put the bed there, Sam looks alarmed and immediate insists that I lower it.

"Try it," I urge. "Just for a little while." He shakes his head. I adjust the bed to 55 degrees for ten minutes, then 30. I stand at the end of Sam's bed and hold out my hands, palms down, waist high, "Can you kick my hands? One leg at a time."

He makes a few kicks. "Good job, Sam!" I give him an Ensure bottle for each hand and get him to do some arm lifts. I am worried that he is losing strength.

The oxygen flowing into his lungs is set at 25 pressure and 40% oxygen by the end of the day with 93% oxygen saturation at his finger.

Things are looking up. Sam is more open, transparent. Less shut down, less frozen. He is glad John is spending the night tonight. He feels comfortable today. His heart rate is slower. He seems calmer and is hearing from God. *Yay!* The respiratory therapist was able to turn down his oxygen levels on the high flow.

"Good job, Sam!"

Sarah has gone to BWI to pick up our oldest daughter Anna, her husband Dan, and little girls, Anika and Pema. Soon they will be here with us! *Such joy!*

Friday, December 21

Sam is doing well on the high flow at 25/40%. He slept well. Is eating well. In good spirits. Did relational exercises with John, Sarah, and me. During the *Listening to God* exercise, I heard God call me "Mighty Warrior" again. God showed me all the ways he had fought for Sam through me. So encouraging.

Saturday, December 22

Sam moved from the high-flow nasal cannula to a regular one. He slept well, ate well and is in good spirits, joking with us all.

I write a haiku at Leadership Development:

> Dad is recovering now
> PCP on retreat
> Smiles. Jokes. Family joy.

The cardiologist says that Sam has not had a heart attack. So much good news!

In the evening we vacate Jerry and Jeannie's home. They are on their way back from Tampa and have family coming in for the holidays. It takes longer than we expect to clean up, wash all the bedding, and clear the refrigerator. At last we lock the door and leave.

I am riding in the back seat of one of the cars. One of my dear ones is upset with me. I try everything I know to do: attune to them, reflect back what I've heard, but it does no good. I try to explain my point-of-view but that makes it worse. They are furious with me.

The urge to flee is so strong the thought of jumping out of the car at a red light flits through my brain, but I remain seated. I have no more words and fall silent. I remember what I learned at Thrive Track Three training in 2016, where we learned that talking only helps conflicts that involve the top two levels of the brain. Lower levels need mirroring, but I can't mirror my loved one from the back seat, and I feel so overwhelmed that I stop talking. This seems to upset them as well, but I don't know what else to do. When I get home I go upstairs, lock the door to my bedroom, and try to calm down. My chest is so tight, it feels as if someone has reached into my chest and is wringing my heart like a sponge. I wondered, *Am I having a heart attack?* I go to bed where I toss and turn all night.

Sunday, December 23

I get up early and drive in from Reston to see Sam alone. Before I leave, I ask Dan if he can take one of his daughters' car seats out of my car.

When I get to the hospital, Sam says he is tired and so am I. I lie down on the bench sofa and we both sleep. I am cold.

"Can I turn up the temperature?" I ask.

"Sure. Go ahead."

I squeeze by several machines to get to the thermostat, pop off the cover and turn the dial a few degrees up. It was set at 60 degrees. I'd been bundling up because his room was cold, but now

I am shivering. I lie down and rest as Sam sleeps a few feet away in his hospital bed.

My phone beeped. "Mom, you took one of the car seats. We can't go anywhere without it."

What was I thinking? Now I am wide awake and shivering. *Am I sick?* I feel exhausted.

Dr. Pic pops into the room to check on Sam. She takes one look at me and pronounces, "You have the flu or a respiratory virus. Go home. Get out of here."

At home, I go to bed.

The next day, Christmas Eve, I stay in bed, too weak to move. I listen to sounds of my happy granddaughters playing downstairs. I am thinking of asking someone to bring me a cup of tea, when I hear the front door slam. A text message beeps: "We have given you the gift of a quiet house so you can rest. Enjoy!"

I feel sad and alone.

On Christmas Day, I lie on the sofa and watch my granddaughters and our guests, some of whom I am meeting for the first time, open presents. Then I trundle back to bed, while everyone eats brunch.

Half of our family has gone to be with Sam, while the other half is home with me.

The rest of the week I rest in bed. I keep thinking that if I take very good care of myself, I will recover quickly. Everyone else has gone back to work or school, but my daughter Anna has stayed on so that someone can visit Sam and help me at home. She leaves her little girls with me. They are both a delight and a challenge. At times I am so weak that I felt desperate, but mostly I enjoy lying on the living room rug while they play with my brio trains, or lying on my bed while they play with nesting dolls.

Soon they are gone, and I am no better, perhaps worse.

Friday, December 28

I am home alone feeling worse. At night, I experienced many apneas, coughing fits, and I am wheezing. I call the advice nurse who tells me to come to urgent care. "Don't drive yourself!" she urges. *Who would drive me?* I wonder. "I have to drive myself," I tell her. "There is no one else."

I get in the car. I have a strong sensation of being led. I pull out onto Route Seven rather than taking the usual route. I sense Jesus is sitting shot gun. *I will direct you,* I hear him say. There are very few cars on the highway, so I drive slowly, holding myself up by gripping the wheel. At times I long to close my eyes, but I sense Jesus strengthening me.

Thursday, January 3, 2019

I've gone in to see Sam. Even though I don't feel well, the doctors say I am no longer contagious. As we sit, the hospitalist and pulmonologist come in. Since before Christmas, they have been talking about releasing Sam, but they keep pushing off the date. "We are going to release Sam," they announce. Then they drop a bombshell. "Since he can't walk much, we are sending him to rehab. Do you have any questions?"

Sam and I look at each other, stunned. We had planned on having him come home. A hospital bed was delivered a few days ago and sits in our family room. "What would be gained by moving him to rehab?" I ask.

"He does not need hospitalization anymore," one of the doctors replies. "The PCP has been killed. Now he needs to recover. He needs to get moving."

I am aware that Sam has been remarkably adept at avoiding physical therapy, or PT. When the therapist comes into his room, he smiles and says, "Not, right now. Maybe tomorrow." Or, "Can you come back in ten minutes?" The result is that he has not had much physical therapy during his stay and is daily growing weaker. Other than my improvised methods—holding my hands out at waist level and getting him to kick my palms—and a few short walks down the hall, he has not been moving much at all. Sammy has gone back to work but still visits frequently. Sarah is back in medical school. Anna and her family have returned to North Carolina.

By the end of the conversation we understand that he is to be moved today, if possible.

A transition coach arrives next and explains various options. We choose a rehab place in Sterling near our home.

Friday, January 4

Sam is going to be discharged from the hospital today. When he entered the hospital, he weighed 205. When he left, only 170. It took so much energy to breathe that he could not keep the pounds on. Prednisone helped keep him alive, but it ate at his muscle mass. If I had not seen him daily, I am not sure I would have recognized him.

He will be moved by medical transport. We know from experience that when it is not an emergency, it can take half a day or more before you are actually picked up and moved. I wait all day for word that medical transport has picked him up and he is on his way.

At last Sam texts me: "Moving now."

I get in the car and drive to the rehab place in Sterling to be sure I will be there when he arrives, but then realize that I am only two miles away, and the hospital is nearly 20. *What was I thinking?* I arrive and sit in the car. It gets cold. I go inside and ask if I can sit in Sam's room. It is the last one, at the end of the hall and I am already losing strength. *Oh Lord, have mercy.*

I sit. An hour later Sam arrives with two paramedics. They help him transfer from the narrow gurney to his bed.

He smiles at me. "Betsy, can you find my urinal?"

I look at him. I am having a hard time sitting up. The idea of hunting for what he needs is overwhelming.

"I've got it," says one of the ambulance attendants. He reaches into a plastic bag and pulls out the handy plastic container.

Sam has more requests for me. The men are gone, so I force myself to do what I can to find what Sam wants, for example, his phone charger. I spend a few minutes ordering his room, hanging up his coat, putting his toothbrush in the bathroom, tucking various items away and bringing those he wants to his bed.

"I need to go home and lie down," I say. I kiss his forehead, then leave.

Saturday, January 5

Sam calls from rehab. They have not given him the medicines that are due at 8 AM, and it is now 10:30 AM. The Bactrim, the antibiotic which he may have to take for the rest of his life, is especially important. He is back on this important drug at a low maintenance dose. The idea that this terrible disease could come back fills us both with terror. I am in bed. I call the rehab place.

The receptionist listens kindly, then transfers my call to a phone that rings and rings. At last it switches over to a voicemail line that has not yet been set up and hangs up on me. I wonder if they send all complaints to this line.

I wonder if I should drag myself out of bed and go in. *I am with him,* I hear God say.

Amazingly Sam has his medicine thirty minutes later. *Did my call help?* I have no idea.

Tuesday, January 8

Sam walked about 300 feet in PT with weights on!

I am still recovering from the flu/bronchitis. I slept in the morning and as the day progressed, I spent short times out of bed. *Am I getting better?*

The federal government has furloughed many people including a friend of mine who offers to help. She rakes and blows our leaves and then gets Mediterranean food for us for dinner. We sit and talk about life.

Wednesday, January 9

From 3:30 to 4:30 PM I visit Sam. He was bathed earlier today for the first time since entering rehab.

My days are spent on the sofa or in bed. I listen to Graham Cooke's *2019: A Year of Promise.*

Cooke says that it is the "unasked questions that trip us up the most."

He suggests asking God, "Lord, who do you want to be for me now?" So I ask.

God responds: *I want to be your provider. Not Sam. Not Sammy. Not Anna. Or Sarah.*

Oh! It is so easy to want to lean on my children, but God is saying lean on him. Help me Lord to lean on you.

I ponder the thought, *it is so easy to want a particular person to help me but God is teaching me to accept the help he brings.*

That night I am even worse, and again at 2:00 AM I drive myself to urgent care in Tyson's Corner. By 3:34 AM the doctor has given me IV prednisone, a new antibiotic (ironically one that was familiar because Sam had taken it in the hospital), a breathing treatment, and a prescription for oral prednisone.

I wonder, *Why are Sam and I having such oddly parallel experiences?* Obviously, he is much sicker and weaker, but both of us are having problems with our lungs. Both are on prednisone and antibiotics.

Thursday, January 10

My friend Chaney texts me: "Worried about you. You need me to sleep there?"

I text back: "Great idea as long as you don't talk to me too much. Talking makes me cough. Doing the nebulizer now, then heading to bed."

"Okay, just finishing dinner, then I'll come," she texts back.

When she gets to my house, she lets herself in, climbs the stairs, and sits on the end of my bed. "I just wanted you to feel loved," she says.

"Ahh. So sweet," I say. "I am glad you are here. Last night was rough."

She has succeeded. I feel loved.

Chaney works each day, but she comes back to my house in the evenings and spends the night. On Saturday a big storm is expected. Chaney leaves in the morning to tend to her busy social life. Before she goes, I ask if she would be willing to come back to my house before the storm hits. She says yes.

At 4:00 PM, she sends a text: "On my way." Snow is just beginning to fall.

We curl up on the sofa to talk, read books, and watch the snow blanket my yard. We get 10 inches of snow and the next day we get even more. I am glad to be snowed in with Chaney. We watch with delight as my driveway seems to be magically cleared. We never see who shovels us out, but later I learn it was my neighbors.

Friday, January 11

Again on the sofa, alone. I hear in my head, *Cloister my heart.*

I wait, then hear more. God is speaking to my mind:

> *I am calling you to be a spokesman for this generation.*
>
> *I am a good father. A good father is stronger, wiser, and more mature than his child. He sees the child accurately. He loves the child deeply. He sees what lies ahead and gives the child the life experiences they need to be able to navigate life well. He is committed to giving the child all they need to prosper. Just like a coach will put an athlete through drills and exercises to strengthen them for the challenges that lie ahead, so a good father is constantly looking ahead and training his child to be able to face the challenges of life well with trust and confidence.*

I am at work in you and Sam. I am training you. I see what lies ahead. I know what is best, for you are my children. Do not be afraid. I go before you. I am preparing the way. Let your hearts be confident in my goodness. You are my beloved children. Trust me. I am not punishing you.

I lie there filled with wonder and awe. It almost feels as if all our suffering is worth the joy of hearing God speak to me so intimately. I feel his presence. Warmth. Love. Peace. Contentment. *God will bring us through.*

Later that day I write to my intercessors:

Dear Ones,

My friend Elaine went to see Sam today in rehab, and she reports that he did well in occupational therapy, walking further than ever before without a walker. He sat up in a wheelchair for at least 45 minutes. He did horizontal and vertical arm exercises—15 with each hand. And he had at least three good "God conversations" with either people who worked there, or who are residents there. Plus, he had a good conversation with Elaine, who finished with these words: "What a super-duper guy!"

Thanks so much for praying for all of us. Today I was deeply touched by this scripture:

Out of my deep anguish and pain I prayed, and God, you helped me as a father. You came to my rescue and broke open the way into a beautiful and broad place. Now I know, Lord, that you are for me, and I will never fear what man can do to me."

Ps. 118:5-6

Love to you all!

B.

Sunday, January 13

I journal my gratitude to God. Lord I am grateful for your clear leading and that you're giving me peace about the fact that I have not been able to see Sam for many days now.

I thank you for the beauty of the snow and that Chaney is staying with me.

> God's response to my gratitude. *I am so glad that even though you are suffering, as you head into week four of bronchitis and Sam is in rehab, you are still maintaining an attitude of gratitude.*
>
> *I see you lying in bed. The air around you is a little cold, but you are warm under the covers. You're a little surprised to find yourself awake at midnight but you're also aware that this is one of the side effects of being on prednisone—a struggle to sleep.*
>
> *You are sad that as of last night, Sam had still not been given a bath since Thursday, and it's now Sunday morning. It seems that some aspects of his care at the rehab place are very lacking. You are trusting me that I am bringing it all together so he can come home. That I am healing you so you can care for yourself and him. I am strengthening Sam so he will be able to walk to the bathroom on his own. You aren't sure if you want him to stay in rehab for twenty days, because then*

he will be released in the middle of the conference. Or if it would be better to get him home beforehand so he can adjust.

I hear you. Just now you had the idea of asking several people if they could help Sam during the conference. You are wondering if you should line up some options or if it's better to wait and see what I do, how things unfold. Your chest feels a little tense when you think about this. You want this season to be over and done, yet when you think about the amazing progress you made in one afternoon on a sequel to Crossroads Before Me, *you wonder if the changes that you are sensing in your spirit are fully anchored, or if you will simply go back to your old ways. You are sensing rightly that I am making some fundamental changes in both you and Sam. I am freeing you from fear. I am giving you confidence in my provision. I am calling you to finish all the book manuscripts you've been writing, but it will happen in my time, not yours. You believe that I'm calling you to simply sit down and grind them out. But that is not my way. That is your way. My way is a lovely dance between rest and relationship and restoration—and serving your husband.*

I am asking you to lay it all on the table. To be willing to lay down seminary. To be willing to consider taking a sabbatical. To be willing to restructure all of HCI. To be willing to spend more time praying and resting. To not be driven by your "to do" list. To trust me more and to know my goodness at deeper and deeper levels.

I am so glad to be with you. I have so much goodness for you. I want to heal your relationships with your children, especially Sammy. Look at what I have already done! You minister to the loved one who was so angry at you in the car, and they have apologized and are now functioning in a way that is so beautiful to me.

You are my beloved Betsy, and I have treasured you since the moment I formed you in the womb. Your childhood was exquisitely painful, but I guided you through from the very beginning and comforted you by giving you the ability to cry easily. Those tears let you shed mountains of pain, and you emerge from the ashes surprisingly healthy yet still deeply wounded.

I have brought you to me and brought you expertise in some of the most powerful methods of healing prayer that I have given our world. As you have ministered to others, you have also received from me in ways that are truly beautiful. You have helped thousands of people and they love you because of your passionate heart for their healing.

You are my secret treasure. Remember the man at Global[9] who prophesied over you? He was disturbed by the level of your humility. He said, "There is humility . . . but you have taken it to an extreme."

You heard his words, but you did not know how to respond. You did not know how to be different than who you are. You still don't understand how someone who is so broken and wounded has come to such a place of spiritual power. You look at Healing Center International in awe—at all the amazing people who have been drawn into the community and all of the amazing things they are doing. You see growth and transformation all around you and you can hardly believe all that I am doing. But I am doing it not only in your community, I am doing it in you. I am fundamentally changing you through your suffering. Through Sam's suffering. Through

[9] Global Awakening Leadership Day.

this snowstorm. I am taking you in a new directions that you do not anticipate and have not seen coming.

You thought 2019 would be similar to 2018, slow progress, healthy growth. Maybe one hundred classes instead of fifty-three, but this is going to be a year like no year before. Not just for you, but for all of your flock, all the ones that you love so deeply and that you so earnestly desire to see grow and flourish.

I am with you in your suffering. I am using it to hold your heart to mine. To make you even more passionate, more holy, more loving and even more able to press in to people who are suffering. You care so much for those who are dying and for small vulnerable children whose needs are not being met. But I am calling you to this generation, the generation of your children. The generation that has been slow to step into HCI.

You are a forerunner. You behaved the way they do today forty years ago when you were in your 20s. You see into their hearts. The distracted attachment. And the parents who are overwhelmed by the intensity of their children's needs and can't think of anything to do other than dismiss and shame them.

There are so many parallels in your life, so many things that you did—such as cohabitate—that they are doing today. You see and have experienced the bitter fruit of this lifestyle. Look at how your article on "Seven Reasons Not to Move in with Your Boyfriend"[10] has spread all over the world and influenced so many people to avoid this trap.

I have more to say to you, but it is for another time. You often feel anxious that you have to wrap something up or it won't

---

[10] https://aredeemedlife.wordpress.com/advice/womens-issues/7-reasons/

get done. But that is not my way. I do not drive you like a herd of cattle. I have seasons for you to turn your attention from one thing to another and it all is accomplished in my time. Look at the manuscript you opened yesterday. There it was. Written so many years ago and yet waiting yesterday for your little edits.

I am always glad to be with you whether you are in a place of joy and gratitude or you are in a place of pain and sorrow. This will never change. You will always be my beloved and I will always want to be with you in every moment. Remember Wednesday night when you were in so much distress, struggling to breathe, experiencing fifteen apnea events an hour for more than two hours. When you got in the car in the cold and began driving to urgent care, I was with you. I led you to drive down your street to Elden and then down Route Seven to Westpark. I remember you asked me to be with you shotgun and I told you that I was actually between you and the steering wheel, driving the car. You asked if you could simply close your eyes and let me take the wheel and I said, No, but I will strengthen you and enable you to drive yourself there, even when the nurse told you not to.

I ordered your steps so that when you got there a nurse was standing next to the receptionist who checked you in. The nurse took you back immediately and within ten minutes you were seeing a doctor who knew exactly what you needed. Within thirty minutes you had had IV steroids, and another breathing treatment. You were much calmer and coughing less.

I knew exactly what you needed, and I brought you to a safe harbor just like a boat on a storm-tossed sea. By morning your chest was open.

I am filled with wonder at what God is doing through this time of suffering. I spontaneously begin to pray fervently for those in our community who are struggling. The Lord brings names to mind and I cry out to him on their behalf. After some time, I hear God say:

All right. I know that you want to go on and pray for everyone, but right now it is time to go back to sleep. I love you and I am with you. You are my beloved and I go before you. I know the way. Do not be afraid.

I roll over and go back to sleep.

Tuesday, January 15

Chaney moved back home on Sunday afternoon. I was sad to see her go but grateful for her time with me. Being alone does not feel so daunting anymore.

But that night I again start having trouble with many apneas an hour. I am not sure what is triggering them, but their frequency make it impossible to settle in to deep sleep. At 2 AM I call the advice nurse who urges me to go to urgent care. *This will be my third trip*, I think. I do not want to go. I ask her to give me the first appointment with my doctor in the morning, instead.

Later I realized I should have listened to her. I thought I would be able to go back to sleep. Instead I was up the rest of the night because I could not get enough air when I lay down.

I wander the house all night, drinking tea, coughing; waiting for the sun to rise. Well before the appointed time, I drive to the medical clinic in Reston. I am looking forward to seeing my doctor. She suggests that I might be overusing my nebulizer. Even though it is early in the morning, she is scrambling to keep up. "I have so many sick patients today," she says. She orders another chest x-ray and puts me on a new, higher dose of prednisone.

I drive home feeling very alone and overwhelmed.

I text a small group of friends saying, "I don't think I can take care of myself."

Silence.

Wednesday, January 16

After I get home from my doctor's appointment, I lay down on the white sofa and hear God saying to my mind, *I am a father to you, and you are my beloved daughter. I go before you. Always. Nothing can separate us. Nothing will ever separate us. I am taking you in new directions that you do not anticipate. Watch and see what I will do.*

Before I forget the words, I use voice recognition to record what I am hearing on my phone. Then I ask, *Lord, do you want to tell me a little bit about where you are taking me? Does it have to do with grief and death? Does it have to do with children? Or making videos or writing books?* I am curious if some of the ideas that have been floating in my brain are part of God's new direction. He does not answer my questions. Instead he continues to speak:

Right now I am showing you that I am your provider. I want you to be confident in my provision.

I grab my journal and write:

> Lord I am grateful that you guided me through a perilous night and brought me to the doctor safely. And that she was able to treat me conservatively.

God responds to my gratitude: *I was with you every step of the way and I did indeed guide you. You are precious to me and you were never out of my watchful eye. I go before you.*

I see you lying on the white sofa. You are spent after a difficult night, and although part of you would like to get something done, another part of you feels like all you can do is lie down.

Last night it seemed that you could not get the house warmer than 65° inside but now it feels comfortable. You are very tired. This has been a long illness, over three weeks now.

I hear you. I hear your parts in conflict: Guardian, who wants everyone to be well and safe and wants to put this difficult season behind him. Function, who wants to do something! At least check email and let people know what happened this morning. Emotion, who just wants to connect with those you love and who is sad that Sam almost immediately hung up after you called him because visitors came into his room.

You are aware that there is some internal dividedness when you're sick. Part of you almost panics and wants to cough to see if you are still congested, to make sure the symptoms are still there and you're not exaggerating. Another part seems to obsess over the symptoms. Then there is a part of you that wants to just relax and trust God and believe that the Lord and the doctors can treat you well without you having to figure it out. It seems that there is a child part there that likes the attention, who feels that somehow it's okay to ask for help when you are sick, and that that is about the only time it is okay to ask for help. There's another part of you that wants to be superwoman and never be weak and never ask anyone for help and always be the one giving and never the one receiving. You are wondering how on earth you are supposed to sort through all this or if you should let it all go.

You don't really like the part that wants attention. You'd rather be superwoman. You are a little stunned at how hard it is to ask for help. You did asked Laura for help last night and she gladly helped to you by driving you to pick up a prescription for more nebulizer fluid.

But then this morning when you thought about calling someone to drive you to the doctor, you choked on it. You texted Nora but she was already at work in Crystal City and when she asked if you wanted Bette to help, you said no. You thought of asking Chaney. Or Elaine. Or even Sammy. And yet you did nothing. It did not feel good to be alone in this. You felt like you barely had the bandwidth to do what had to be done—drive to the doctor's office, get out and come inside, stand in line to check in. Even though you were the very first in line. You had to go downstairs to get an x-ray and wait in line there. You pulled the end table over so you could sit on it while you waited in line for your x-ray. Came back upstairs. Let them know that you were back. Picked up your new prescriptions, including a new nebulizer. And then of course drove yourself home. You would much rather have had a girlfriend or Sam with you to help you.

"Lord, why I do feel conflicted about asking for help?" I ask.

You are afraid you are asking too much. In your culture it's not OK to ask for too much.

Later that day I get word that they are going to release Sam from rehab. I wonder how I will take care of him when I can barely take care of myself.

Thursday, January 17

Sam is coming home today!

It is hard to imagine how it is all going to come together. He needs medical equipment, and so far all we have is a bed and an oxygen concentrator, and a few oxygen tanks. It seemed chaotic, out of control. I am lying on the white sofa, wondering if I should make some calls. But I have no strength to make it happen and I sense God telling me to trust him, so I simply lie on the sofa and trust.

Sammy is bringing Sam home. The night before, I realized that it would be better for Sam to enter the house through the garage which has only two steps into the house rather than the front door which has three. But the garage is full of boxes of Christmas decorations, as well as a car. Sam needs a clear pathway from the driveway to the house wide enough for a walker. I put out a plea on Facebook. No one responds, so after an hour I call my neighbor. He has 45 minutes before he has to leave for another appointment, so he comes right over and moves enough boxes, brooms, and mops to make a path through the garage.

Then we need a walker. The doorbell rings and a kindly man delivers a walker! I cannot imagine how Sam would have made it from the car to the house without it. I am so relieved.

I text Sammy: "Got the walker! It's all lining up!"

His immediate response is: "We're almost there."

Yikes!

The night before, an oxygen vendor had delivered an oxygen concentrator and set it up in our family room, but then it broke as he demonstrated its use. He had another concentrator in the truck so he brought that one in—a much larger, more powerful unit—and said he would be back the next day to swap that one out.

Suddenly the Prius is in the driveway. Sammy is helping Sam out of the car. I bring out the walker. Sam moves at a snail's pace down the driveway and into the garage. At the house door, Sammy closes in behind his dad and hooks his hands into the door frame to support him as he steps into the house. I wheel the tank of oxygen behind. Sam lands heavily on the hospital bed a few steps inside the door and lies down, exhausted.

Once Sam is home, the doorbell continues to ring. First a home health nurse, then the oxygen vendor, then a man to service our heat pump, which is badly in need of care. It seems like a three-ring circus.

I am still suffering with bronchitis and asthma and my strength begins to fail. *How am I going to take care of Sam and myself?* I sense God saying, *Let Sam take care of himself.* As I listen, I get a picture of how I can set up the area around Sam's hospital bed, so he can take care of himself. *But did I have the bandwidth to make it happen?*

When we are finally alone, I ask Sam, "Can you use the bathroom? Can you do this for me? I know it is easier to lie in bed and use a urinal, but the bathroom is about twelve feet away and I know you have walked that far in rehab."

Sam looks a little confused. He says it is easier for him and I know that. Then he agrees to try.

"I am going to set up everything so you can take care of yourself," I say in a tone that I hope is encouraging.

He looks doubtful. "Are you going to give me my shots?" He needs a shot to the stomach every day for the next seven days.

"No," I say kindly, "I am not." Then I have to leave the room, because the thought that I am a terrible wife is assailing me and I am about to cave. That first night I help Sam with the confusing lists of prescriptions.

We are going to need help, I think. I phoned my friend Nora to see if she can come. I have benefited from her organizational skills before. She comes Saturday morning to get a sense of the situation, then goes out to buy trays, drawers, and file boxes. She shows us different options and helps us set up the ones we like.

We end up with a large tray that sits on a coffee table near Sam's bed. It holds the nebulizer, a box of Kleenex, a blood sugar kit, and a thermometer—and some chocolate! We hope the tray will keep things from falling on the floor where Sam cannot reach them. A little set of plastic drawers on wheels holds all his medicines sorted into drawers and bags. He can push it out of the way when he needs to use the walker to get out of bed, but it is still within reach. We have fabric bags sewn by Nora's friend that we can tie to the bedrails to hold his phone. And a charger looped through the bedrails. A small file box holds the bewildering array of paper work that the different vendors have handed us, as they bring equipment into the house: bed, walker, oxygen tanks, oxygen concentrator. As well as paperwork for the home nursing and home PT. Paper from Kaiser, the hospital and rehab. So much stuff!

We spend the entire day sorting through paperwork and Sam's medicines, which are quite complicated, involving pills that have to be swallowed, a nebulizer mask and solutions, an inhaler, a pill that needs to be taken under the tongue, a shot that has to be given in the stomach. Medications that are taken daily, twice-a-day or "as needed." Medications that are on a taper where the dose changes each day. We make huge progress, but there is still more to do. Our goal is to get it all set up into a system of checklists, where everything is within Sam's reach, so he can take care of himself. We have a list of what Sam must do each morning:

check blood sugar, do nebulizer, do disc inhaler, shots to stomach, eat breakfast, take oral medications, and take sublingual medication. Sam looks a little overwhelmed when we get it all set up, but by day two he seems to enjoy taking care of himself.

It is a good thing too because our conference starts on Tuesday. A few weeks ago, I wondered if I would be able to attend. I have already given Sam's slot away, sadly. But he does not seem to mind and is happy to be home.

My friend Nora helps me make up the bed in the guestroom for our conference speaker. She notices that the quilt needs to be washed, and we stick it in the washing machine. She simply rolls up and takes away an area rug that Darby has peed on at some point! I am so grateful that John and Judy are taking care of our dog because we don't have the capacity to take care of ourselves—much less him.

Friday, January 18

I hear from God, *I want you to write about life as it happens.*

Later than morning I start thinking about Sammy.

I know he wants to talk, but when I think about talking to him, I feel hopeless, certain I wouldn't be seen or heard or understood. I text him to ask, "Can I write you?" I want to write so I can carefully choose my words, let them sit for a while once I have composed the letter. Make sure I am not triggered and that my relational circuits are on before I send it.

He texts back that he would rather talk. I know that, but I don't think I can. I am afraid of what I might say, what he might say. Afraid I will say things I regret and poison our relationship. When he agrees to get a letter from me, I start writing. I describe specific instances where I felt dismissed. Where I was accused of being overly negative. Exaggerating. When I finish, it is a long letter. I let it sit a few days and read it again. I soften the tone. Then I send it.

I think about the quote I saw on a construction wall at LAX years ago: "One frequently finds their destiny on the road they have taken to avoid it."

I have been avoiding open conflict by leaving the room when I am upset, hiding my vulnerability. All this has accomplished is distance and hard feelings between me and those I love. And it is not over yet.

Sammy goes silent. I text him, "I love you."

He texts back, "I know. I need some space. I love you, too."

I give him space. I understand that my words may have landed on him like falling bricks.

Now Sam is upset with me for upsetting Sammy. I know this is true, but I am going forward the only way I know how. Clumsily. I believe I have to speak up, but I am sad that it is causing pain.

Right after I send the letter, I email my intercessors. I want to be sure we are covered in prayer. At 3:05 AM I send this:

When daylight comes, I need to take Sam to the pulmonologist. The thought of getting him to Tysons Corner seems daunting, but we have talked through various options and have a plan. Our friend Bill is going to drive, so he can drop us off in front of the medical center. I plan to run inside and get one of the "loaner" wheelchairs I have seen before parked near the entrance. Sam assures me that he can pull the oxygen tank in its cart with one hand, while I push him in the wheelchair (he had done this before in rehab).

Everything goes according to plan. At first. I get the last wheelchair in the lobby and roll it out to Bill's van to fetch Sam. But Sam and I are only ten feet inside the medical center when the oxygen tubing that extends from Sam's nose to the tank gets tangled in the wheels of the wheelchair. I tug and pull, then do something I am not sure I have done before. I cry out, "Help, help!" Two security guards immediately jump to our assistance. Their strategy is to pull hard on the tubing. I am afraid it will break, leaving Sam without oxygen, but then Sam asks me to back up the wheelchair, and when I do, the brakes release and the tubing comes loose.

We have one oxygen tank with us in a rolling cart and once he had parked the car, Bill meets us at the pulmonary clinic door with another one. We had been told by the nurse that at Sam's high rate of use, the tanks would only last an hour. As it turns out, the pulmonology clinic has tanks that they can switch you to once you are inside. It is a relief to know that will not need to lug two tanks of oxygen with us every time Sam has a doctor's appointment. We also learn that the Kaiser wheelchairs have racks under them designed to hold tanks of oxygen, so we will not need to bring the cart.

The nurse tests Sam for stamina by having him circle around the hallways on oxygen and off. He is pretty amazing and does lap after lap even as his oxygen saturation drops. They conclude what we already know—that he has to be on oxygen. He also gets a chest x-ray that will serve as a baseline for future visits.

The doctor explains that the pneumonia is gone but that it had left Sam's lungs injured. Now they will need to heal. This can take up to a year. It is impossible to predict how much healing will happen in the year. Probably most healing will happen in the first few months.

We are encouraged to hear this. It had been easy for both of us to think, *Yikes, three weeks have gone by since Sam left the hospital and, yes, there's been quite a bit of improvement but not as much as we would like.* The idea that there will continue to be improvement over the next eleven months is encouraging.

The pulmonologist also says that it is absolutely crucial that Sam not get the flu. He says, "Lie low." This has great appeal, because we both feel worn out by what we've been through.

God has been saying he has me in a new season, that I am a race-horse, and have been running for so long. I'm near the point of collapse, and that he wants to slow me to a walk.

Later that day a box of Monk Fruit is delivered to my door. My sister, who lives in Toronto has urged me to try it. I open the package to find twelve hairy balls, like miniature coconuts. I call my sister. Her Asian friend is there, and they walk me through making tea from a hairy ball. Soon I have a pot of dark brown liquid.

"How much do I drink?" I ask.

"Keep drinking it until you stop coughing," they reply.

This is hard to imagine. I've been coughing and coughing for weeks. I drink and drink.

It works!

Later I check with my daughter in medical school and she looks it up. Clinical trials show it is a natural anti-inflammatory. I urge Sam to drink it, too, since his lungs are also inflamed.

Sunday, January 20

Our conference speaker, Dr. Karl Lehman, is arriving this evening at Dulles. I am concerned about potential delays because Chicago, where he lives, is supposed to be hit by a snowstorm. I am confident that he's going to make it out, but not sure of the timing or my strength, so I devise a back-up plan if his plane is delayed and I email it to him. I send him instructions on how to get to our house by Uber, as well as how to find his room in our house if I have already gone to bed when he arrives. I try to think of everything. I send him a map of the airport and the all-important detail that the door numbers outside and the baggage claim numbers inside are in opposite order. I had flown the same airline before and knew that he is likely to come out door five.

He is only staying with us one night. During the four-day conference he will be staying closer to the venue.

I'm improving at last, though still fatigued. I can only be up for so long, then back to bed. Still coughing, wheezing. But all of this is so much better than a few days ago. I am sleeping without using the cough syrup with codeine. I learned from Sam's pulmonologist on Friday that that is probably the source of my dizziness, so I'm determined to stop using it.

Sam has been stricken by debilitating anxiety each morning since he got home. This makes him breathe fast and shallow.

He's unable to move just four feet from the bed to a chair at the table. It's hard to watch him struggle. I want to both help and fix him. Meanwhile the food I've made him gets cold, and his oxygen numbers slowly drop. The first day I patiently waited, and it only got worse. I eventually turned up his oxygen flow. I wasn't sure if that was the right thing to do. Then I ran upstairs and got Sam's three-ring binder of appreciation moments and began to read them aloud. *That helped!*

Later that day I asked the pulmonologist if it is okay for me to turn up Sam's oxygen and he assured me that it is OK for me to do that.

Saturday morning, I find a recording on our website that I made a year ago that leads one through a breathing exercise. That seems to help, too.

Last night Sam and I talked about the fact that when he sits on the edge of the bed and waits, it only gets worse, and that it would be better for him to simply move from one spot to the other without checking his oxygen saturation over and over again.

But this is potentially risky as he could faint or fall.

At one point he forced himself to move and he did fall, but thankfully he fell back onto the bed.

I tell my intercessors what is going on and ask them to pray for us. I share our ups and downs, our joys and sorrows. I thank them for holding us before the throne of God.

I recognize that when Sam is overwhelmed, he shifts into a freeze state. This is unfamiliar to me, as I tend to fight or flee, not freeze. I'm not sure how best to help him return to joy. *This is going to be amazing when we master this skill!*

It's hard to see Sam so vulnerable, so anxious. I get anxious, too.

In the afternoon, I journal with God:

> Gratitude to God: I am so grateful for Monk Fruit tea! I feel so much better. Natural anti-inflammatory.
>
> God's response to my gratitude: *I love Monk Fruit tea too! I enjoyed creating it. When I made it, I saw you drinking it in 2019!*
>
> You are such an amazing God, able to take in the scope of history in a single glance.
>
> *I see you sitting at the kitchen table. Your stomach is full of smoothie. You are drinking Monk Fruit Tea. Sam is in bed doing the nebulizer. His blood sugar was 106 and he seems cranky.*
>
> *You awoke in such a great mood. Excited about the Sabbath. Wanting to do Stalcup Family Church at home and journal. Excited that Sam is home! Now you feel your spirits sinking.*
>
> *You are trying to get back to joy before you slip into hopeless despair.*
>
> *I hear your fears, your distress. You long for connection. While you were at the table eating, Sam was staring blankly ahead, out in space. He did not want to eat with you. He wanted English muffins when all you had was wheat toast. He did not want the sausages you prepared, and he prefers another kind. Right when you ran out of strength, he wanted breakfast. Now. He probably won't eat the ripe strawberries you put out even though you dusted them with sugar.*

Why am I trying so hard? I wonder, and this thought comes into my mind: *I am trying to make things perfect, because somehow I believe that perfection will protect us.*

Oh Lord God, help me! I cannot save Sam. I cannot fix Sam. I cannot make him keep his blood sugar low. I cannot make him more flexible. I cannot make him drink Monk Fruit tea. Or want to eat the food I have prepared.

I remember his father. Inflexible.

I hear your distress. I am glad to be with you right in the middle of it.

Lord there is a tight pain right in the middle of my chest.

I know. I feel it too.

For a moment I ponder the reality that God feels what I feel, even in my body.

I continue talking to God. "Lord, would you open the prison doors holding the pain and trauma and all the effects of the pain and trauma and let it flow to you? I am releasing it to you, my sovereign God. Please take it from me."

I sense the pain leaving my body and flowing to Jesus. I am relieved I cannot overwhelm him.

I hear him speaking to me again. *No one fully appreciates what the other offers. Sam does not appreciate you, and you do not appreciate him. You were distressed at living alone, but you grew to appreciate it. Rooms stayed tidy. There was no dirt on the stairs. There was very little laundry. Almost no cooking or dishes. You lived simply and rested.*

I wonder, *What do I appreciate about Sam? He is kind-hearted. He is compassionate. And demanding.* Smile.

God continues: *Sammy wants to be there for you, but he does not have the capacity to do so. You are similar. You want to reach the whole world and help everyone in pain but that is my job, not yours.*

Your craving to be understood, validated, and acknowledged has deep roots. No one will ever understand you like me, for you are a prophet. No one will validate you like me, for I see what is true and I share my heart with you. I alone see your heart, the sacrifices you are making. You simply must turn to me. I have hemmed you in behind and before. I am Yahweh. There is no other.

Later that day I check the weather. The storm had hit Chicago, but it looks like Dr. Karl's plane is only slightly delayed. Just 15 minutes after the scheduled arrival, he calls me from the plane, "Is it too late? I can take a cab."

"No, no!" I reassure him. "I am on my way." I circle once. On the second circle, I find him and soon we are headed home. As soon as we get to my house, I take him to the family room, where Sam is resting in his hospital bed. While they enjoy getting to know each other, I head up to bed. I am glad that I have already explained where everything is, so Dr. Karl knows how to get a snack and find his guest room without me.

Monday, January 21

In the wee hours of the morning as I lie half asleep, the thought comes to me: *Could I somehow host a dinner party for Dr. Karl and my four friends, who are coming in from out of town for the conference?* My friends are arriving about 5 PM. I had not planned to have my friends and Dr. Karl overlap. *Could it work?* I do the mental math; it would only be seven people. *But was I up for it? Was this my idea or God's?*

I consider going out to dinner, but that would leave Sam, the consummate extrovert, home alone. My guests are all arriving at

Dulles around five. I had texted them each other's flight info and suggested they meet at the airport and Uber over together.

Could I make dinner for seven in my weakened state? *Is this you, God? Or me? If you want me to do this, can you show me how?* The ideas unfurl like a carpet before a king. Order food from Costco, which has just started delivery service in our area. I could put fresh chicken in a crockpot and prep the rest of the food in stages. I am not completely confident, but I am excited!

I make a grocery list in my phone and go back to sleep.

The morning is glorious. Sun on patches of snow and the trees casting lines of shadows. Sam calls me to come down when I am still in bed and, thinking his need is urgent, I fly down the stairs in my flannel pajamas.

Dr. Karl has just seen the fox that lives under our deck when there is snow on the ground. "A fox!" he says. "A big one." I beam. Someone else appreciates the fox, who indeed has unusually long legs.

Since I am downstairs, I cook sausage and eggs for the men. At breakfast we talk about the day. Dr. Karl wants to sit in our sunny living room and go over his talk. I want to make sure we go over my list of potential volunteers for the demonstration sessions. I had sent out an email and had a list of about ten volunteers.

Right after breakfast Dr. Karl and I sit on the white sofa and go through my list, person by person. He listens and asks a few questions such as, "Where are they stuck?" I feel my heart sink. I do not have answers. In vetting them, I had focused on the degree of experience, not the issues they were facing.

Then he says, "For the advanced sessions I would like to work with someone who has dissociated child parts."

Without thinking, I let what is in my mind roll off my tongue: "I wonder if I should volunteer. I have had a child part surface during Sam's illness. And I am pretty triggered."

"Tell me more," he says.

"I think it is a dissociated child part that has disorganized attachment."

"REALLY!" he says as his eyes widen. He leans towards me. "That would be perfect! We could demonstrate the eye-contact tool and the . . ."

I hold my hands in front of my face, palms out, and instinctively say, "Back off!

He immediately lowers his intensity, but I bolt like a frightened colt up the stairs. *What am I doing?* I ask myself. As I climb, I call back, "I need to take a shower. Let me think about it." But even as I reach the stop of the staircase, I can hear the hope rising in the heart of my distressed child part. *She is hopeful of help from Dr. Karl,* I realize. I can feel her settle down at the thought that help is on the way. She is quieting and no longer making such a ruckus. *How can I let her down?*

During the course of the day, Dr. Karl is kind and attuning. I calm down even more. Midday, as I prepare lunch, I tell him, "I am warming up to the idea."

Still thoughts occasionally intrude. *Am I strong enough to sit up for an entire session? Will the intensity of receiving ministry in front of 140 people leave me completely depleted?* Of course Dr. Karl reassures me I can say no, but I am ready to sign on. We tentatively agree that I will be the demo on Friday, the last day.

I place the Costco order online and go back to bed. It arrives while I am sound asleep, and Dr. Karl puts it in the refrigerator. When I get up from my nap, I put the chicken in the crockpot and prep the Brussel sprouts while sitting at the kitchen table. I ask Dr. Karl—the only able-bodied person in the house—to fetch the leaves for the table from the basement, then go take another nap. While I am napping, he puts the leaves in the table single-handedly, all while going over his slides.

At 6 o'clock the rice is done, the Brussel sprouts ready to be roasted, and the doorbell rings. My friends are here. Such joy to look into their smiling faces and feel their warm hugs. Sam gets out of bed and eats with us. My heart sings. I can see him come alive in the presence of our beloved guests.

At 7:30 the family with whom Dr. Karl will be staying comes to pick him up. As soon as we say our good byes, I show my four friends where the sheets and blankets are kept. They make up their beds and do the dishes while I get Sam settled for the night. We are all in our rooms and the house quiet by 8 PM. *Thank you Jesus, you ordered our steps! We are grateful.*

Tuesday, January 22

In the wee hours of the morning, I sense the Holy Spirit giving me very specific directions about how to take care of myself during the conference. I had already planned to take a camp bed (a thick inflatable mat) with me, but now Jesus is showing me that I should also take a thick knit afghan and a small pillow.

One of our house guests drives us there in my car. When I get there, I find a spot against the wall on the side of the sanctuary and lay out my bed, then find a seat nearby.

It isn't long before I am finding it very difficult to sit up. I feel self-conscious, but I know that it is my job to take care of myself, so I lie down. I can see the speaker from my prone position and am comfortably warm and cozy. Even so, by noon I am questioning if I my set up is going to work. I feel over-stimulated and need deep sleep to be restored. I do not have the capacity to listen to the talks even while lying down. It feels unbearable. Like my chest is going to explode.

My friend Sarah notices my distress, and asks the conference host if there is a little room I can lie in. The pastor of the church lets me use the sacristy, where the communion elements are prepared, and the priests put on their robes. It is immediately to the left of the platform. My friend David moves my bed, afghan, and bag for me. Then he moves all three chairs for my practice group to the other side of the sanctuary to a spot right outside the sacristy. This is perfect! Whenever I need to shut everything out and sleep deeply, I simply step into this room, lie down, and sleep.

From inside the little room, I can hear a shift in tone from the speaker's cadence while lecturing and the buzz that ensues when people are getting into their practice groups. I am able to participate in all of the small-group exercises with my group. And I have the perfect group of people with whom to practice, close friends who are very safe. I still experience waves of respiratory distress, coughing fits, and debilitating fatigue, but every time, by God's grace, I make it through.

People are incredibly kind. At lunch, I go straight to the front of the food line because I don't have the energy to stand in line. Everyone accommodates my weakness graciously.

The conference is sold out, the room packed. Walking through the room is like trying to get from the parking lot to the surf at the beach on a crowded day in July. We have to weave our way through and around nearly fifty clusters of three chairs.

The method we are learning is about interacting with Jesus in every aspect of our lives. Dr. Karl is an incredibly dynamic speaker—winsome, kind, Christlike. I have only been around him one time before in 2011, and from what I experienced in our home and what I saw during our conference, he has undergone a dramatic personality transformation. I tell him this, "Before you impressed me as a brainy geek. Now you seem so much more relational and Christ-like." He agrees and says that others have made similar observations. I ponder how spending time with Jesus transforms every aspect of who we are.

Our friends are the best houseguests ever. They are attentive to Sam. They make eggs just as he likes them. They cook. They clean. One woman even fixes my dishwasher and changes the setting on the hot water heater. In the evenings I go home to Sam, and within minutes our friends arrive with dinner. Every night there is a different collection of people around the table. It seems that God is orchestrating each one of us so that we have sweet times of community with each other and others at the conference. Sam and I feel so loved!

In the weeks and days before the conference began, each one had asked, "Should I get a hotel? We don't want to burden you." But I had simply said, "Please come. Come and be with us. Come and help." And they did! They are incredible.

While we have been away from Sam during the day, many friends have come to bring him lunch and visits. He has had just the right level of support: one visitor in the morning, one visitor in the afternoon.

Thursday, January 24

This morning on day three of the conference Dr. Karl asks me, "Who is going to be the demo today?" Even though I know the advanced training will be starting this afternoon, I am surprised by the question. I thought we had already decided that I was going to be the demo on Friday and Maria was going to sit in the hot seat on Thursday.

When I question him Dr. Karl tells me, "You can go whenever you like."

Hmm. I instantly realize that it would be much less stressful for me to go today. It seems silly, but I am nervous about having Dr. Karl work with me on stage. I look for Maria to ask if she has a preference.

"Do you mind if I go today?" I ask.

"Not at all. You are welcome to go first."

My body fills with joy. Now I don't have to fear being vulnerable in front of everyone—*at least not for long!* The demo will be in less than two hours! Less time to be anxious. Every time I begin to get nervous, I hear God say, *Don't think about the session. Don't even think about what embarrassing things might surface, or if you'll say something unkind about a loved one. Just let Dr. Karl lead.*

Before I know it, they are fitting the microphone to my face.

The first thing I say to Dr. Karl is, "I can't believe I let you talk me into doing this." The audience laughs and I laugh with them. I feel the tension leaving my body.

The session is unbelievable. I am in the hands of an expert who is ready and willing to attune to me right where I am. We talk briefly about my experience of not being heard or seen when I knew Sam had pneumocystis and no one believed me. I remember the sting of being told that I was "overly negative" by my loved one.

Dr. Karl coaches me to focus on a positive memory. The one that comes to mind is the fox in the woods. I see that Jesus was excited to bring me and Dr. Karl together. He knew we were both nature geeks. I see Jesus with me on the blue sofa in our family room. We have our feet on the coffee table. My little girl feels that this is very naughty, but Jesus assures her that it is okay, "We have our socks on and we can wash the glass top later." We enjoy the view out the window to the woods. The sun is shining. Sam cannot see us easily in his hospital bed since we are further back and off to the side. I feel like I am playing hooky from fetching and carrying. Jesus is looking at me, glancing down when I glance up. Our eyes meet, and we giggle. I can feel that my heart is very tender. Jesus tells me, "I can take care of your tender, scary feelings."

In the presence of Jesus, it is safe to see that the intensity of Sam's suffering and my being misunderstood has dislodged a buried child part of me that has disorganized attachment, the most insecure kind. The little girl may have been right about Sam's diagnosis, but she did not know how to communicate without becoming shrill. The Lord speaks to her about being confident about what she is hearing him say. Jesus and Dr. Karl validate the little girl, which she loves.

But she is also angry and now that her feelings are being met with empathy, the pain comes roaring up. It is a little scary to see the intensity of her emotions. In that moment I think, *I have enough emotional intensity to overwhelm the whole world. If anyone gets in my way, I will mow them down! If people see this part of me, they will run! I deserve to suffer. I got triggered and lost it. I have to stop being so negative and exaggerating.*

All of this pours out of me. It is overwhelming to see what that part of me believes.

Dr. Karl reflects back, "So your negative emotions are so big everyone will run away?"

"Yes, I will overwhelm even Jesus."

"Jesus is that true?" he asks.

No, Jesus answers to my mind. *I can handle your intense emotions.*

Now I am aware that I have not one but two child parts. One carries anger, another fear.

"What would you like me to call the angry part?" Dr. Karl asks.

The name "Sasha" pops into my mind. *Where did that come from?* I remember that I often use countries as examples of attachment styles with Russia being the example for disorganized attachment. Is that why I chose that name?[11]

We go through the memory of Sam being moved to ICU. Flashbacks of this scene have been waking me in the middle of the night. I begin to experience Jesus with me in those places of trauma. He is jogging alongside me, his hand on the small of my back, attentive to my distress as I clutched the top of Sam's bedrail. Jesus is with Sam, too.

I ponder the wonder that Jesus can be with every single person in the world at the same time.

I see Jesus encouraging me. *Don't give up. Don't let go of the bed or stop running.* I see us roll the bed into ICU, and the nurse steps forward to ask me to give them ten minutes to get Sam settled. I see myself telling her that I cannot leave him, but that I promise not to interfere as I step into his room. I see Jesus with the nurse

---

[11] Later I learned that Sasha means defender of mankind. Was it prophetic?

helping her back off and let me do what I have to do. I see that Jesus has given me courage to speak up and not give in to her request.

I see myself standing against the wall watching them transfer Sam with amazing precision from one bed to the other. I see them put the mask on Sam's face and the machine force air into his lungs. I remember calling out to him, "I'm here, honey." I remember the absolutely frantic look in his eyes.

I see Jesus with us, holding us up so we do not collapse. I see Sam settle down as oxygen fills his lungs. I see him falling asleep.

I see me asking if they could simply leave us alone and let him sleep. I see that Jesus was the one who gave me that idea and the courage to speak up. I remember them looking at me. They did not say anything, but they turned out the lights and left the room.

I remember pulling up a chair and stretching out my arm across Sam's feet, and putting my head on the bed. At that moment, I knew I could take my attention off my frantic husband and rest. I see that Jesus has orchestrated everything; he has put the words in my mouth and given me the courage to stand up and not collapse in a puddle of tears when people were not supportive of what I knew I had to do.

I had been so afraid at the thought of Sam in ICU, but it turned out to be a haven of safety. The first 24 hours, Sam had his own nurse. His anxiety declined because they finally started treating it. They had told us earlier that medicines for anxiety would slow down his breathing and were contra-indicated, but they can do things in ICU that they cannot do on the regular floor.

My memories of a traumatic time are transformed as I interact directly with Jesus. I feel as if loose pieces of me are being woven together into a beautiful tapestry. By the end of the session, both of my child parts are in the arms of Jesus, completely happy.

That night as I lie in bed, the one thing that feels unresolved is this question: *Lord, did I really need to suffer so much? It seemed over the top.* It was crazy that I could not get Sam to go to the doctor, and that when he finally went, the doctor misdiagnosed him. It was absurd that I could not get him to go back. It was searing to have the medical team tell me that this kind of pneumonia is often fatal and then hear them say, "If only we had gotten him a week earlier!"

It was excruciating to see my husband frantically struggling to breathe, hour after hour.

And on top of all the suffering of Sam's illness, members of my family were critical of me, claiming I was overly negative because I thought from the onset that Sam had pneumocystis pneumonia.[12] It turned out that I was right, but they never came back and said, "You were right. We accused you of being overly negative, but you were actually right, and if you had not insisted that the pneumonia had to be related to the bone marrow transplant, Sam could have died."

What's more, I had fallen ill myself. It was the perfect storm of pain.

In the middle of the night I made my complaint to God: *Was it really necessary to make me suffer so intensely? You asked too much of me!*

---

[12] Looking back, I realize that I was negative about more than just the pneumocystis diagnosis. My fears made me see many aspects of the situation negatively. But in the ministry session this was what hurt.

What he told me completely swept away my accusations. I saw that he was right there with me every step of the way, slowly turning up the heat, incrementally, to the precise level of intensity. He knew exactly what degree of suffering I needed to experience for those two child parts to surface. I had had so much healing, but there was more. It was as if my capacity for suffering was at a nine and Jesus took me to a ten. He said, *The size of your suffering had to be the same magnitude as the size of your wounding so that the wound could be exposed and healed.*

In a moment, I shifted from complaining to awe. God is with us in the fire. He knows what needs to happen to expose our brokenness, and he is so committed to our restoration that he is willing to suffer with us so we can be free beyond anything we could ask or imagine.

In a flash I gained even more insight: those two child parts of mine were very active when my kids were young. Back then I was working on my PhD, trying to prove myself as a scientist. I was chronically under stress, much of it self-imposed by the high expectations I placed on myself. Those child parts were shrill, upset, and demanding, and took control whenever tensions rose.

The intensity of Sam's illness brought them to the surface again, and, of course, they triggered my adult children! *They recognized them!* They had been traumatized by my gang of two: fear and anger. From my point of view, it felt like they had turned on me in the midst of the crisis. Now I could see with compassion what had triggered them too.

I pondered this reality: in a life and death situation, everyone in the family will be triggered. Little tensions that we have tolerated will rise to the surface like a rogue wave and knock us down. We have to expect it and keep going to God. He is the only one with a clear perspective on what is transpiring.

I recalled something I often tell our community: you have to practice the exercises[13] on your good days, so you will have them on your bad days.

I saw with new understanding that Jesus is with us in our suffering, feeling what we feel, all the while carefully watching to make sure that what we are experiencing is intense enough to surface what needs to be healed, and yet not so intense as to completely shatter us. I saw my heart enter into a new place of trust in God. I saw that he was very attentive to what I was experiencing, down to the tiniest detail.

Jesus allowed our entire family to suffer up to a certain boundary, and he protected us from going over the edge. He felt what we felt, experiencing all the intensity with us. He was not willing to let us suffer needlessly but had a purpose for every ounce of blood wrung from our hearts. We were not being punished. We were being healed and set free.

Also, immediately after my session with Dr. Karl, I could feel that my chest was much less tight. Emotional and spiritual healing was healing my body too.

Thank you, Jesus!

I was so tired the next day that I spent almost all of Friday lying on my camp bed. In the afternoon, I started coughing a lot and I thought I might have to go home, but I managed to get through by drinking mug after mug of tea.

---

[13] For example, quieting, appreciation, Lectio Divina, Immanuel Journaling—all the spiritual exercises we practice at HCI.

We had a sweet team dinner afterwards. At 8 o'clock I told the group that I was fading and needed to go home. There were hugs all around and my friend Sarah drove me home.

At home another dinner party was breaking up. Friends from the conference had brought Sam dinner and companionship. I was able to visit briefly with everyone, then I remembered that we had not heard back yet from the pulmonologist whom Sam had seen on January 18th. Ten days had elapsed. I asked Sam to check his phone. There was the message: "The x-ray of your lungs on January 18 looks much better than the one that was taken in the hospital on December 28. You're improving. You're headed in the right direction."

With great joy I called out to all the people who were still in my house "Hey listen to this!" as I read the good news aloud.

It had been a great week for me, one of great victory, and a great week for Sam, too. On the very first day of the conference, Sam decided that if he was going to recover, he had to make decisions a hundred times a day to do hard things. When he told me his resolve, my heart leapt for joy.

That day he determined to stay out of bed the entire day! This was a huge shift. The physical and occupational therapists at both the hospital and rehab had asked him repeatedly to try to spend more time sitting up, but he had resisted. But the first day of the conference, he stayed out of bed the entire day (other than a nap) and once he started spending the day sitting up, he did it every day from that point forward. I was so proud of him for pushing himself. I knew that sitting up was much better for his lungs as well as his entire body.

With a smile on my face, I headed to bed while the dinner party guests were still in the house. I no longer felt that I had to entertain everyone. It was okay to take care of myself and let them take care of themselves and Sam.

As I drifted off to sleep, I realized that it would've been easy for me to think that I needed to stay home from the conference and take care of Sam, but that was not God's plan. Being away caused him to rise up and take more responsibility for his own health.

God knew exactly what needed to happen and he brought it all together in an amazing way.

After the conference was over I called my now adult children and apologized to them. I explained about the two child parts who had surfaced and how sorry I was for the way I had behaved when they were little. They readily forgave me.

Recently my son Sammy said, "We have such a great relationship now!"

I agreed. I felt that the relationships in my family have never been better. Yes, indeed. Thanks to God who does all things well.

Afterword

On February 14, 2019 David and Jan Takle announced "An Urgent Call to Prayer for Betsy and Sam Stalcup." Thousands of people prayed for us, our extended family, and Healing Center International from sundown on February 15 to sundown on February 17.

We saw many things shift during the vigil. Here are a few:

1. Sam's anxiety left. No longer on Xanax and no longer anxious. We consider this a huge answer to prayer. He is quiet, cheerful, and working hard.

2. Sam has had an epiphany. He said, "I realized I've been quite resistant . . . to going to the doctor."

3. I am feeling more confident. I am also seeing my tendency to amplify when I don't feel heard and am committed to being more accurate.

4. During the prayer vigil, I heard God tell me to finish several manuscripts I have written but never completed. I am on it! This is one of them! Prayer appreciated here!

5. I am praying more, and praying more in depth. Sensing God saying, *Your prayers are powerful. Sometimes that is all you need to do: pray.*

During the vigil, God began speaking to me about many things he is calling me to do. Things that seemed *waaayyy* beyond me. Then he gave me visions of waterfalls: Yosemite, Niagara, Vernal. God showed me that we can be so close to amazing power and not perceive it. It seems so tranquil at the top. Yet water is powerful, and stunningly beautiful as it falls.

He said:

> *You don't have to do anything that does not bring you life. These are lessons from the waterfalls. What I am calling you to will be as effortless as water going over the falls. When the time is ripe it will happen. In the same way, I am preparing you now, helping you to finish your books.*
>
> *It is the falling water that creates the energy. The water cannot help but go over the edge. Follow my leading. I know the way. I am leading you out of the lake and over the falls. You will be my spokesperson.*
>
> *I have hidden you in me, to go deeper with me, to learn of me, to write.*

Like a seed that is buried in the ground, at the right season it will emerge and bear fruit. Your job is to get ready.

I am leading you; you cannot go astray.

Woe to you when all men speak well of you because you are saying what they want to hear. You are to be a spokeswoman for me. My mighty warrior. There is a battle. I want you to be confident. Be not afraid. Speak my words, not what people want to hear.

Then I asked God to heal Sam and he said: *I am healing him, but it will take a long time. Abraham received the promise, but it took a long time for Isaac to be born. Trust me. I am doing much more than healing him physically. He will be the head of a mighty nation.*

Thank you for reading this slice of life from Betsy Stalcup, Executive Director and founder of Healing Center International, where we share the joys and sorrows of life with joyful leaders who know they are loved by God. **You can find out more at www.GodHealsToday.org.**

48987495R00052

Made in the USA
Middletown, DE
20 June 2019